YOUTH IN CELL
MINISTRY

Youth in Cell Ministry

Discipling the Next Generation Now

JOEL COMISKEY, PH.D.

www.joelcomiskeygroup.com

Copyright © 2017 by Joel Comiskey

Published by CCS Publishing
23890 Brittlebush Circle
Moreno Valley, CA 92557 USA
1-888-511-9995

Cover design: Jason Klanderud
Editor: Scott Boren

ISBN: 978-1-935789-85-7
LCCN: 2016902742

All Scripture quotations, unless otherwise indicated, are from the Holy Bible, New International Version, Copyright ©1973, 1978, 1984 by International Bible Society. Used by permission.

CCS Publishing is the book-publishing division of Joel Comiskey Group, a resource and coaching ministry dedicated to equipping leaders for cell-based ministry.
Find us on the World Wide Web at www.joelcomiskeygroup.com

PRAISES FOR
YOUTH IN CELL MINISTRY

"One of the most exciting things that is happening in cell churches around the world is how thousands of young people are being discipled and also being trained as leaders! As I read the manuscript of this book, I became so fascinated with the depth in which Joel Comiskey deals with one of the most important subjects in church life: "What is the best way to truly be effective in discipling the next generation?" I can't wait to have our main lead pastors and youth ministers devouring this book!" **(Abe Huber, principal leader of the Igreja de Paz movement, Brazil)**

"When Joel undertakes a cell group topic, you know you're getting a thoroughly researched resource, filled with practical ideas and proven strategies. As a former Youth Pastor with a groups-based ministry, I can tell you that Youth In Cell Ministry is a fully loaded toolbox for any leader that is serious about discipling the next generation"(**Andrew S. Mason, Founder of SmallGroupChurches.com**).

"This is one of the most exciting books I have ever had in my hands. You can not lead cell ministry without empowering the members to evangelize. But the content of this book goes beyond evangelism. The biblical perspective of youth ministry is clearly articulated in this book. I love working with young people, and I believe that youth work invovles more than youth services. Youth need a much larger cause for living. Empowering them is a debt we owe to the future of the church. I have been inspired by Comiskey's investigation. The stories here are inspiring and the dynamics are typical of all of Joel's books. I recommend this book to all who can see the potential of young people and want to disciple them in cell ministry" (**Jorge Peña, founder and lead pastor at iRest, Reseda, California**).

"Church is not a sail boat; it's a war ship. Our young adults have understood that and pastor Joel realizes that God is moving through young people around the world. The church's greatest pastors are still to be developed" (**Josué Bengtson, pastor and apostle of Belem Foursquare Church, Belem, Brazil**).

"Joel begins with the *why* and then moves into the *what* and *how to*. This progression is vital for the *why* is seeing youth know Jesus, become disciples of Jesus, and then to plant churches throughout the world. Joel writes, "One important goal of this book is to help readers analyze, research, and prepare to reach youth in their particular culture—to become cross-cultural missionaries where they live and work." Because "everything rises and falls on leadership," Joel encourages youth pastors to guard their mind, heart, and soul. Finally, wherever you or your church family are regarding youth cells, I wholeheartedly recommend this comprehensive, informative, visionary, and uplifting read" **(Rob Campbell, founder and lead pastor of Cypress Creek Church, Wimberley, Texas).**

"With a great Biblical underpinning and powerful, real-life testimonies, Joel Comiskey unveils a clear vision for youth cell ministry. I am inspired again with the incredible opportunity the church has to reach the next generation. I recommend this book to anyone who is wanting to not just "baby-sit" young people, but raise them up to be disciples of Jesus!" **(Robert Herber, Lead Pastor, All Peoples Church, San Diego California)**

"Joel has been an incredible help to our church in regards to cell ministry. I love his passion for seeing young people come to know Jesus and become disciples. I am thankful for his thoughtful leadership on the why and how of discipling youth through cell ministry. This book will show you how" **(Zach Daniel, Lead Pastor, Antioch Community Church, Dallas, Texas).**

TABLE OF
CONTENTS

ACKNOWLEDGEMENTS

I'm very grateful for those who have contributed to the writing of this book.

Anne White spent a lot of time thoroughly copy-editing the final manuscript. She excels at finding grammatical errors and untangling faulty sentences. I also appreciated her timely comments about the book's content, and it's always a joy to work with her.

Once again Jay Stanwood helped me simplify complicated sentences and then suggested straightforward solutions. He gracefully offered suggestions and helped me to rework paragraphs that didn't make sense. Jay's contributions made the final version much better.

Bill Joukhadar took the time to look at the final version, and I appreciated his effort.

Scott Boren, my primary editor, guided me to understand the big picture and how to organize the material. He took a very rough draft, bogged down in quotes and detail, and helped me to look practically at the big picture. His expertise guided me throughout the process, and I'm very grateful for his editing.

I'm very thankful to the pastors and leaders who consented to interviews and questions about youth ministry. The following leaders contributed their insight to the making of this book: Joel Sanders, Blake Foster, José Abaroa, Brian Sauder, Vinicius Motta, Thayana Machado, Mario Vega, and Armando Pavón.

INTRODUCTION

John Alves accepted Jesus when he was eleven years old in a children's cell group at the Vine Church in Goiania, Brazil. Soon afterwards he attended a spiritual retreat called "Encounter" and God healed him of bronchitis. After baptism at the age of twelve, he began a discipleship course which eventually led him to lead a youth cell group, which he multiplied three times.

As he coached the multiplication leaders, God placed a calling in John's heart to become a pastor. He received various prophetic confirmations, and in 2011 he entered the church's equipping for future ministers. After two years of equipping, John became a fulltime pastor overseeing a network of youth cell groups.

John is now twenty-four years old and one of the thousands of pastors and missionaries from the Vine Church who were discipled as young people and now in ministry. The Vine has a razor sharp focus on discipling the next generation and a clear path to make it happen.

The good news is that the Vine Church is not alone. Many churches, including the ones highlighted in this book, are effectively discipling youth and preparing them for future ministry. This book describes how churches do this and why cell group ministry is perfectly suited to disciple the next generation for Jesus.

MY JOURNEY

I began following Jesus in September 1973 when I was seventeen years old. A few months later, I was in a small group that met on the Millikan High School campus in Long Beach, California. I learned to pray out loud in the group, and there was freedom to ask questions. God's Word became alive to me as I interacted with others. I had a place to go when I was discouraged and a team to help me live the Christian life on the Millikan campus.

When I was nineteen, I started leading a cell group of predominantly seventeen to twenty-three years olds who met in my parents' house. We grew together, experienced trials, debated theology, discerned false teaching, and most of all developed deep, lasting friendships. We learned to overcome conflict, love one another in practical ways, and allowed God's Spirit to work among us. This was our group, among our own peers, and we felt like God was speaking to our generation each week in the cell group.

Bob Burtch was the co-leader who also led worship. Because we were good friends, I accepted his critiques of my Bible messages, although they were hard to take. I didn't know much about God's Word, but I shared what I knew, and God poured more into me. Often my teaching was shallow, but the cell group was more than my Bible teaching. We shared life together and grew spiritually as we challenged each other.

One evening we invited Ginger Powers, a missionary smuggling Bibles into East Germany, to speak to us. Her words and vision impacted all of us. Through her words, God lit a fire in my heart for missions. As a nineteen year old, I was ready to go with her to Germany, but God had other plans. I didn't realize that a career in missions might require more preparation than simply packing my bags and leaving North America. I eventually did leave our cell group to participate in a short-term Youth With A Mission trip, which led to Bible college, and eventually career missions. Although the group sent me off, we gathered together for fellowship during my Bible school breaks, and even to this day, I maintain contact with some of those original group members.

Jesus himself chose the small group atmosphere to prepare his disciples. He spent time with his young followers, interacted with them, and taught them to love one another. He then said to them, "All authority in heaven and on earth has been given to me. Therefore go and make disciples of all nations, baptizing them in the name of the Father and of the Son and of the Holy Spirit, and teaching them to obey everything I have commanded you. And surely I am with you always, to the very end of the age" (Matthew 28:18-20). The disciples knew exactly what to do. They started home group ministries that multiplied and changed the Roman world. And home cell groups are just as essential for disciple-making today.

MAKING DISCIPLES

When Jesus gave the Great Commission to his disciples, they knew exactly what he meant. After all, Jesus practically demonstrated it. Jesus developed his own group of twelve and shepherded them for three years. In that cell atmosphere, the disciples were molded, shaped, trained, and then sent forth. These same disciples became the key leaders of the early Church.

Not only did Jesus minister with these disciples over the course of three years, but he then sent them into homes to establish house churches that would multiply and infiltrate the surrounding communities (Luke 9 and 10). In other words, house-to-house ministry in small groups was the way Jesus made disciples, and he expected his disciples to do the same. The houses or apartments were very small in the ancient world, and they were excellent meeting places for making disciples.

Small groups are still the best training ground for future disciples. Jose Abaroa, youth minister at Cypress Creek Church, in Wimberley, Texas, challenges his young people to become disciples by leading small groups called *community groups* on junior high and high school campuses. He expects a lot from his youth, and they have responded by leading and multiplying their groups. The campus junior high cells meet right after school on Wednesdays for one and one-half hours. The groups are dynamic, fun, and empowering. Those leading the groups grow more than those attending as they are challenged to trust Jesus to use them. Jose confidently believes that his students are capable leaders and can effectively minister to other students, while becoming disciples in the process.

Jose also gathers the youth cells together on Sunday as a congregation. "They need to know we're going to be there for them," he told me. Jose is passionate about cell ministry because he himself was born again and discipled in a Cypress Creek community group meeting on campus at Texas State University in San Marcos. Jesus transformed Jose in the community group, and he wants others to experience Christ in the same way, including the junior high and high schoolers. Some react negatively to the word *disciple* but the original meaning simply means pupil or learner.[1] After Christ's resurrection, the word disciple was broadened to include such words as *believer, saint, Christian,* and brother or sister in Christ. Why? Because after Pentecost, God established the Church, the gathering of believers, to be the main place where discipleship occurred.

Youth cells are an exciting way to make followers of Christ who are molded, shaped, and transformed in the process. We'll discover in this book how churches disciple young people through cell groups and larger youth gatherings. We'll see how churches transition to youth cells, avoid common mistakes in youth ministry, and even plant youth cell churches to make disciples worldwide.

.

_____Chapter 1_____

BIBLICAL BACKGROUND FOR YOUTH MINISTRY

Around the world, God is transforming youth through cell ministry. Grace Fellowship Church in Hong Kong develops missionaries through youth cells and sends them to unreached people groups all over the world. The Elim Church in El Salvador is turning violent gang members into disciples of Jesus through youth cells. As gang members receive Jesus, they become part of a true, spiritual family—something they had only dreamed of finding through the gangs. York Alliance Church (YAC) in York Pennsylvania is connecting youth with adults through their intergenerational cell groups. In the process, YAC has connected the young with the old and established a mentoring process that continues after college.

What God is doing today with youth reflects the biblical pattern of God's work in young people from the earliest pages of Scripture. God has always prioritized youth and so should we.

GOD STARTS WITH YOUNG PEOPLE

The names of Moses, Joshua, Abraham, Joseph, Ruth, and David are familiar to Jews and Christians alike. Pulpits worldwide proclaim these men and women of God who are found in the pages of the Old and New Testament. Their names also appear in countless Bible stories in Sunday schools, adult Bible lessons, and even in the secular media. We call them heroes of the faith. They fuel our imaginations for what God can do and challenge us to become like them.

We often overlook, however, that God called these men and women as youth. As young people, God worked through them, tested them, and then moved them on to greater influence and leadership positions. Through their testimonies, we're reminded that youth is an opportune time period for God to start the discipleship process. God loves to do the unexpected through youth and to challenge the false beliefs that only the older and wiser can be God's special tools.

Joseph, was a "young man of seventeen" when God interrupted his sleep with some amazing dreams (Genesis 37:5). God eventually used Joseph to save the world from starvation and deliver his family, the bloodline of Christ, to prosperity in Egypt. Joseph listened to God and remained faithful for the twenty-two years that it took for the fulfillment of those dreams and the saving of many lives.

Joshua was Moses' aid since "youth" (Numbers 11:28). When Moses interceded with God in the Tent of Meeting outside the camp, Joshua would go with him. After Moses received the message to pass onto the people, "his young aide Joshua son of Nun did not leave the tent" (Exodus 33:11). Joshua's strong leadership was developed through the many years Moses mentored him. Joshua's influence can be seen by the fact that Israel continued to live for God even after his death: "Israel served the LORD throughout the lifetime of Joshua and the elders who outlived him and who had experienced everything the LORD had done for Israel" (Joshua 24:31).

Samuel is another excellent example of God's calling to young people. We read that the "boy Samuel ministered before the LORD under Eli" (1 Samuel 3:1). He first heard God's voice and call as a child. When Samuel was "old and gray," he testified that it was from the time of his youth that he was a leader for the people of Israel (1 Samuel 12:2).

Ruth was still a young woman when she became a widow and followed Naomi to Bethlehem (Ruth 1).

David was a mere boy when he defeated Goliath and attracted the attention of the king. David's character development and faith exploits began when he was a boy shepherd, caring for the sheep (1 Samuel 17).

Josiah was king at the age of eight, and by the time he was in his late teens, God used him to bring a rebellious nation back to God (2 Kings 22:1).

Daniel and his friends were probably teenagers when they were led across the Fertile Crescent into captivity. We can imagine them as young men, quite possibly in their late teens, as they testified to Yahweh and interpreted the king's dreams (Daniel 1-5).

Solomon says in Ecclesiastes 11:9, "Be happy, young man, while you are young and let your heart give you joy in the days of your youth." Solomon concludes in Ecclesiastes 11:9-12:1 that the ultimate goal of life is to "remember" God while you are young and can still determine the course of your life. Many adults have become entangled in the affairs of the world, missing the peace and joy of following God wholeheartedly and living according to his truth.

Mary, the mother of Jesus, was a mere youth when the angel appeared to her with unprecedented news of her supernatural pregnancy (Luke 1:26-38).

Some have observed that Jesus led the original "youth group," believing that Christ's twelve disciples were probably under the age of eighteen.[2] Christ's choice of the twelve gives new meaning to youth ministry and motivation to disciple those who are young.

The Apostle Paul first began to work with Timothy when he was approximately sixteen years old. Paul discipled Timothy and developed him to become the pastor in Ephesus, a very important church. He exhorted his young disciple, "Don't let anyone look down on you because you are young, but set an example for the believers in speech, in conduct, in love, in faith and in purity" (1 Timothy 4:12). He then told Timothy, "And the things you have heard me say in the presence of many witnesses entrust to reliable men who will also be qualified to teach others" (2 Timothy 2:2).

RELATIONAL DISCIPLESHIP

There are over fifty direct references to the one anothers in Scripture, exhorting the Church to love one another, care for one another, confess faults to one another and so forth. These one another passages confront individualism, help Christ's Church reflect the character of the Trinity, and combat increasing depersonalization. Youth, like the Church in general, are called to reflect God's relational, triune character. Youth cell groups provide an opportunity for young people to experience face-to-face interaction and become relational disciples in the process.

Many youth, especially in the western world, experience deep loneliness. They go home to an empty house, where they are raised by the flickering blue parents called TV. They spend hours and hours alone in the little kingdoms called their bedrooms. More than any other generation, today's young people have had to raise themselves without benefit of meaningful relationships.[3] Youth cells provide those intimate relationships—friends with whom they can talk, listen, and share life. Seasoned youth worker, Ron Hutchcraft, says,

> The number-one priority for modern young people is relationships. They will do almost anything to get one—and then to keep it. When a young person gets something that looks like it might be a decent relationship, he or she will pay almost any price for it. Relationships have become number one because deprivation creates value. Whatever you are deprived of is what you tend to value.[4]

And it's through these intimate connections that youth experience healing. When Charles entered the Saturday night youth cell for the first time, it seemed so strange to receive a hug and to hear the words "welcome home." His mother never gave him a hug, nor mentioned the phrase "I love you." She worked twelve hours each day in a "sweat shop" factory and had little positive energy to impart to her children. His dad, a construction worker, had not been around for six years.

Normally on Saturday night, Charles would go out with friends and smoke pot and take drugs. At sixteen Charles had developed a drug habit and was smoking pot several times per day. Yet, something happened that Saturday night in the cell meeting. Charles heard the good news of Christ's death and resurrection and the possibility of living an abundant life here and now. The youth cell leader seemed to be talking directly to Charles, and he realized that he needed to change.

Charles tried to resist the cell leader's words, but then something unexpected happened. The youth leader came and sat by Charles saying, "Jesus knows your sadness and is willing to help, as long as you will let him." In that moment, Charles couldn't take it. He broke down, weeping uncontrollably. He nodded his head informing the leader he wanted to receive Jesus to wash away his sins and sadness. "A tremendous peace came on me," Charles said. "I felt like a weight was lifted from my shoulders." Charles felt love for the first time in his life as those in the youth cell embraced him, welcoming him to the family of God. "For the first time," Charles said, "I felt like I had a purpose in my life." Since that day, the youth cell has become a new family, a new home.

Never again did Charles use marijuana. "I was even disgusted by the odor of marijuana," he said. He also developed a deep love for his mom, dad, and brothers and sisters. "The Elim Church is my new family, and I will continue to fight for my entire family to experience Jesus Christ, just like I have," he said. Charles found a family through the cell group, a place to grow spiritually, and is in the process of becoming a disciple of Jesus. Relationships are at the heart of Christ's incarnational ministry. Brian Sauder, co-author of the book *Youth in Cell Ministry*, writes,

> For real change to occur in teens' lives, especially in our postmodern world, kids have to experience, hear and see truth before they will believe it. In the small relational setting of cell groups, kids can be given responsibility and encouraged to take responsibility for their lives. They can learn to love God and find healing for their deepest pain.[5]

Learning to submit to one another and practice humble service to each other pleases God because this is how the three persons of the Trinity relate to one another. Youth all over the world are being transformed to be like God through intimate connections in the cell.

YOUTH MINISTERS

Effective youth cells expect everyone to be a minister. They embrace the apostle's exhortation in the last book of the Bible, "To him who loves us and has freed us from our sins by his blood, and has made us to be a kingdom and priests to serve his God and Father—to him be glory and power for ever and ever! Amen" (Revelation 1:5-6).

This is one main reason why Jesus chose the small group atmosphere to impart knowledge to his own youth cell. Christ wanted the information to be disseminated into the lives of his disciples, so as he journeyed with them each day for three years, he not only taught them, but asked them to interact with others and apply his teachings. Sometimes Jesus would allow them to make mistakes in order to teach them important lessons and offer practical application of his teachings (Matthew 14:22ff).

Young people hear many sermons, but those messages are often difficult to apply until they are discussed. Small groups allow for discussion about how truth can be implemented in students' lives. For example, if the church teaching is about witnessing for Christ, a student in a small group can talk about particular ways he can share Jesus with his classmates. The teaching moves from an impersonal, platform presentation to the small group and into the student's lifestyle.

Many youth are not challenged. They are caught up in the vicious cycle of low expectations. They are not asked to do the hard things. No one expects much of them, and they even expect less of themselves. Cells are uniquely positioned to challenge youth to grow in their faith, develop relationships, disciple other youth, and reach a lost world for Jesus.

Alex and Brett Harris wrote a successful series of blogs called *The Myth of Adolescence* that eventually turned into a bestselling book entitled *Do Hard Things: A Teenage Rebellion Against Low Expectations.* They point out that teens desire deeper meaning and should be challenged to fulfill their dreams [6]

The Holy Spirit is able to do amazing things through young people who trust in him and are willing to step out. A cell church pastor in Africa, referring to student leaders, said, "While they may be young the Holy Spirit in them is no child." The same Holy Spirit works just as powerfully in youth as he does in adults.

Thayana, one of the youth pastors over cell groups in a Foursquare church in Belem, Brazil, is helping to break the mold of traditional youth ministry and showing others that youth can accomplish a lot. Thayana led her first small group at the Foursquare church in Belem when she was fourteen. She excitedly talked about Jesus at her school—inviting her friends to her cell group. Her group led so many people to Jesus and water baptism that in one year it had multiplied into two groups and then two more the next year. By the time she was sixteen, she already had five small groups under her care. When Thayana was nineteen, she became one of the network pastors. There are now more than 200 small groups from the one she started. She personally supervises a network of eighty-three cells.

Thayana is exceptional in her leadership and coaching skills. She is also in a church that allows youth to thrive. All Christians are encouraged to actively participate in cell ministry. In fact, youth cell ministry stands against the idea that only the youth pastor does all the work while the rest of the youth sit and listen—and perhaps engage in a few programs.

Participation is at the core of the cell. No one sits as a spectator only. As youth share their stories, ask for prayer, and minister to one another, they are transformed in the process. They become the ministers and grow as Christ's disciples. The best cell leaders, in fact, empower others. They are facilitators. The word *facilitate* means to *make easy,* and the best facilitators make it easy for others to participate. They unwrap the gifts and talents of those in the group. They only talk some thirty percent of the time and encourage those in the group to speak the remaining seventy percent. Talking, of course, is only one aspect of cell life. Participation is far broader and involves active engagement in each part of the cell group.

GIFTED YOUTH

The gifts of the Spirit are freely given to all, regardless of age, gender, or race. 1 Peter 4:10 tells us that all those born of the Spirit have at least one spiritual gift. Youth, in fact, are prime candidates to use their spiritual gifts because they abound with energy and are ready to practice what God has given them. They expect God to move and unlike many adults, have not become hardened and limited in their thinking about God's power and willingness. Kara Powell writes,

> There is no Scriptural evidence that gifts are given to believers at a certain age. Rather, they are granted when any child, teenager, or adult surrenders his or her life to Christ. The church, Christ's ongoing body, requires its members of all ages to exercise these gifts in order to remain healthy and productive (1 Corinthians 12:14-20).[7]

Antioch Community Church, based out of Waco, Texas, began as a youth movement on Baylor University campus and now plants churches worldwide, focusing on young people who in turn will reach a lost world for Jesus. It is not a traditional Pentecostal church, but they do encourage youth to use their spiritual gifts. My 22-year-old daughter, Nicole, recently opened a high school group at an Antioch Church in Fullerton, California. She describes her experience,

> Each youth that walked through the door at the life group was in tears during worship as we prayed over them, spoke prophetic words over their lives, and listened to their hearts. One student's head was healed, another girl decided to give her life to the Lord fully for the first time, and all were deeply touched by Jesus.

> At the end of the night, one of the students began
> weeping and declaring that, "Surely, this was the start
> of a youth movement!" The weeks that followed were
> just as supernatural as the students began to minis-
> ter to each other. We walked away each week more
> amazed at the beauty and power of God.[8]

In the cell group, each person plays an essential role. In fact,
those who have a more visible role are not more important. The
parts that are unseen are given special honor. The body needs
each other to be healthy and whole. The goal is for everyone to
participate, discover their gifts, and minister to others.

God sets youth in his supernatural, organic body according
to the gifts of the Spirit (1 Corinthians 12-14). In all three
of the major passages in which Paul talks about the body of
Christ, he defines each member's part in the body by their
corresponding gifts (Ephesians 4; Romans 12; 1 Corinthians
12-14). The teaching that the Church is the body of Christ
is to remind the Church that every believer is valuable and
esseWntial and needs to exercise his or her gifts.[9] Those in the
early New Testament church had the opportunity to interact
among themselves as they met in house churches. They grew
together as disciples as they exercised their spiritual gifts and
ministered to one another.

Small groups are an ideal atmosphere to experience God's
power, discover spiritual gifts, and minister to one another.
The Spirit-filled small group, in fact, was the "normal" church
in the New Testament; it was never seen as an "addition" to
the "real" church. The small group was the church. These
small house churches would meet together in a larger group
for corporate celebrations whenever possible, but the small,

Spirit-filled house churches were the main vehicle through which Christ's body grew in the New Testament period.

Effective youth cells and youth cell leaders make disciples in the same way Jesus made them. The cell is small enough to mobilize each person and to get them involved in using their gifts and talents. Ginny Ward Holderness echoes this, "Experience has shown that young people will be actively involved in youth ministry if they have ownership in it. They need to feel that youth ministry is theirs, that whatever happens at their church belongs to them. They need to own it, drive it, and care for it."[10] When the group is small and intimate, people are confident to participate because of face-to-face involvement.

GENERATION TO GENERATION

My good friend, Daphne Kirk, runs a ministry called *Generation to Generation*. She believes that preparing the next generation is God's major emphasis in Scripture and his primary objective in the Church today. As the Psalmist declared, "One generation commends your works to another; they tell of your mighty acts" (145:3-4). Not all generations are successful in doing this. The generation that followed the Exodus of Egypt, for example, "knew neither the LORD nor what he had done for Israel" (Judges 2:10). Their parents failed to instill in their children the true knowledge of God and his great acts.

Reaching the next generation compels youth ministry. It's the zeal to pass on God's truth to those who will be the leaders of tomorrow's Church. Paul's plea to Timothy to pass on his knowledge to faithful people is what youth ministry is all about (2 Timothy 2:2). Each generation must be taught who God is and what he has done for humanity. It's false to assume that future generations will fully embrace Christianity because their parents were Christians. The reality is that faith tends to dissipate and lose its excitement in the next generation.

Prioritizing the future generation means preparing youth now. Just as New Testament house churches developed future leadership in a warm, intimate setting, the cell provides an ideal environment to develop the next generation. There are many youth right now who could change the course of history in our cities, countries, and nations. God wants to give us a new vision for making disciples of youth in order to equip them to change the world and reshape the future.

_____Chapter 2_____

A MISSIONARY CALLING

My wife and I were missionaries for eleven years in Quito, Ecuador. Like Jesus coming to this earth, our goal was to become good news in a culture which spoke a different language and had customs and mannerisms far different from our own. We studied hard, failed a lot, and learned to enjoy the process. Youth ministry is a lot like foreign missions. Those working with youth need to learn another culture and relate to a people with different hopes, aspirations, and needs.

Blake Foster leads the junior high and high school youth ministry at Antioch Community Church (ACC) in Waco, Texas. He became a follower of Jesus at twenty-six years old as a freshman at Baylor University and was discipled at ACC. When he graduated from Baylor, he prepared to pay off his loans and go to the mission field. In fact, he and his wife both felt a call to missions and were considering going to the Middle East to spread the gospel. Youth ministry was never on his mind until the college pastor asked if he'd be willing to consider it. He and his wife took time to pray and fast. During that time period he received a prophecy about walking through the open door and felt God was calling him to say yes.

Up to that point, Foster was accustomed to ministering to young adults, not youth. But God showed him that the younger youth were his new mission field. As I interviewed Foster, the phrase "cross-cultural missions" came up again and again. "I see my friends on Instagram, and at times I wish I was ministering to those of my own age group," Foster said. "Yet, God has called me to my new mission field of young people." Foster realized that he couldn't effectively minister to the youth half-heartedly. It required total immersion. "You have to be involved heart and soul. You can't do it half-heartedly. You have to be restless to allow God to enlarge your territory and your own heart. You have to be willing to weep with those who weep and rejoice with those who rejoice."

UNDERSTANDING YOUTH

Each culture will define youth a bit differently. Youth in San Salvador, El Salvador, face unique problems, like gang warfare. Youth growing up in the high-tech culture of Orange County, California, face challenges such as busyness, materialism, and indifference. Like missionaries, those working with youth need to study their target audience. No doubt, some youth pressures and characteristics are similar to all youth everywhere but even those similarities are constantly in flux. One important goal of this book is to help readers analyze, research, and prepare to reach youth in their particular culture—to become cross-cultural missionaries where they live and work.

The term adolescence comes from the Latin root word adolescere, "to grow up," and is most often used to describe puberty to adulthood or maturity.[11] The word teenager didn't come into vogue until the early 1950s and comes from popular culture. Mark H. Senter III explains,

> The word teenager was a product of the World War II era. Apparently first used in the magazine Popular Science in 1941, the moniker was quickly adopted by the world of advertising to label the demographic group between thirteen and nineteen years of age. The war prematurely transformed older youth into adults, claiming their efforts either in the armed services or as support in the war effort through employment for vital industries. This left high school students and their junior high school counterparts as a unique group. They became that distinct group called teenagers.[12]

Youth normally starts at age thirteen until the person takes responsibility for his or her actions. Most cultures would agree that youth ends when the person turns into a responsible individual who is no longer dependent on parents. But there is also the question of age brackets. For example, those who are thirteen to sixteen years old have different needs than those in the seventeen to twenty-one age bracket. Those working with young adolescents should be sensitive to their level of maturity, not thinking they are developing faster than they are.[13] The age of the youth will also determine how much adult supervision is needed. Junior high groups, for example, need a lot more adult attention than senior high school groups or those who have graduated from high school.

Becoming a missionary to youth involves discovering the core rules that motivate youth to behave the way they do. Steve Gerali, expert in the field of adolescence and youth ministry, writes,

> Being like adolescents involves immersing oneself in their culture. When missionaries go to foreign fields, they learn the languages, customs, practices, traditions, and values of the people they are trying to reach. To fully understand the community, they must bring those practices into their home. They speak the language within the context of their family so that they adapt to the community. They practice the customs and traditions so that they can relate to the people. They become all things to all men so that they might save some.[14]

Just like missionaries who learn a language and culture, those effective in reaching youth need to get involved in the social world of youth. It involves understanding and experiencing those things that affect youth today. The best youth missionaries know adolescents better than adolescents know themselves.[15]

BECOMING GOOD NEWS

God himself became incarnate in the Roman world of the first century to become good news to that culture. Scripture tells us that the Word became flesh and dwelt among us (John 1:14). Missionaries do the same thing. Those who want to become good news to youth must know their heartaches, what they are struggling with, and how God's Word resolves those particular issues.

When my wife and I arrived in Costa Rica in April 1990 to become fulltime missionaries with the Christian and Missionary Alliance, we longed to speak Spanish correctly because we knew we'd soon be missionaries in Ecuador. As we studied the Spanish language, we learned that God gives grace in weakness. Instead of saying, Quisiera conocerte, "I would like to get to know you," I would say, Quisiera cocinarte, "I would like to cook you." Some of my more hilarious Spanish blunders are not repeatable in public.

I began to learn Spanish when I was thirty-three years old. Sorting out the foreign Spanish sounds was difficult for me. To compensate for my lack of natural talent, I had to study for hours. Like a child, I learned the importance of following grammar rules and the logic of the Spanish language. I knew, however, that taking time in the beginning would have a long-term impact on my ministry in Latin America.

Then we had to learn the customs and culture of Ecuador. I wrote long papers on Ecuadorian culture, trying to understand the people I was going to reach. But ultimately we had to live among that culture and get to know the Ecuadorians. All our research and study were insufficient. Only after actually living among the Ecuadorians year after year did we really learn their customs, culture, and heart-felt longings. We often learned through the trials of making mistakes, being corrected, and then repeating the process. Slowly we began to feel confident that we were making headway and reaching our people in their heart language.

The size of the gulf between youth and youth worker depends on the youth worker's age, background, or upbringing. But the gulf always exists. While youth workers must not appease cultural norms that result in straying from the biblical message, it is important to set forth the biblical truths in ways that make them appealing to youth.

Joel Sanders, youth pastor at All Peoples Church in San Diego, highlighted a volunteer in the church who became a football coach at the local high school to better relate to those he was trying to reach. This same volunteer began leading a youth life group and a Christian club on campus. "He cares for the youth and they know it," Sanders said. "He's gained their trust by getting to know them and being their friend, and the youth love him."

And getting to know today's youth requires time. Troy Jones, Assembly of God youth minister, believes that it takes six years to really get going in youth ministry.[16] His point is that those ministering to youth need to spend enough time to learn what makes youth tick. It's far too common for youth workers, whether volunteers or paid, to move on too quickly.

GOING DEEPER

The book *Blind Descent: The Quest to Discover the Deepest Place on Earth* is a fascinating story about cave exploration. Author James M. Tabor vividly illustrates how the best cave explorers push deeper into the caverns, tapping on walls, going under streams, and crawling through cracks to find entrances into caves. The best youth ministers are not satisfied with superficial communication, choosing rather to lovingly probe deeper to get to know the youth better and grow in a long-term commitment where relationships flourish. Cross-cultural missions among youth is similar. Duffy Robbins says,

> Youth ministry is a cross-cultural ministry. It requires people of one culture (adults)—with one set of values and mores regarding fashion, leisure, volume of

music, and so on—to cross over into the world of another culture (teenagers) with its distinct language, customs, arts, and preferences."[17]

Blake Foster's ministry to youth at Antioch led him to conclude that one of the biggest problems facing his people group, the youth of Texas, is communicating with others. "The youth go through conflict but they are unable to articulate their battles to anyone else," Foster said. "They also struggle with face to face communication. They might be able to send a text to someone, but they struggle to be real and vulnerable to people." Foster realizes that youth in the U.S. spend about 7.5 hours per day multi-tasking on multiple media devices.[18] A large part of the face to face communication problem stems from countless hours interacting with impersonal devices rather than real people.

And of course, online media and its impersonal way of communicating isn't just a North American problem. Youth around the world are becoming more connected via the internet, whether living in China, Argentina, India, Europe, parts of Africa, or the U.S. Those ministering to youth need to keep this in mind and reach them on their turf—one that is deeply influenced by the internet.

Ultimately the best way to reach youth is through the love of Jesus and by encouraging youth to get involved in ministry themselves. Foster said, "Until the young person is actually practicing what he or she has learned, growth is sadly limited." And involvement can be messy. Youth don't grow up in isolated, private spaces. They do it publicly, and their actions can turn off adults who forget about their own problematic upbringings. Eugene Peterson writes,

Adolescents are, more than anything else, growing up.
They do not do it quietly. They do not stay in their
rooms and grow up in isolation; they do not restrict
their growing to the times when they are safely among
peers. Their growing spills out, unsystematically, all
over the place. In this way adolescents energetically
modeling and constantly stimulating growth, are
God's gift to parents who are in danger of being
arrested in their own growth.[19]

Those who are committed to loving and understanding youth
will discover effective ways to win them and become good
news in the process.

WINDOW OF OPPORTUNITY

God is actively working among youth today. In fact, research
has shown that somewhere around eighty-five percent of
people who make a commitment to Jesus Christ are making
that commitment before the age of eighteen, and those who
don't make the commitment by this age probably never will.[20]
Ron Hutchcraft rightly says,

There is a bottom line that has driven me for more
than thirty years in ministry. At least three-fourths of
all those who ever accept Jesus Christ do so by the
age of eighteen. When you go to the local high school
graduation and watch the kids walking across that
platform, realize that those who don't know Christ
then will probably live and die and spend eternity
without Him. The church of Jesus Christ has nothing
more urgent to do than reach people before their lives
turn hard—while they are young.[21]

Youth ministry is an important time to reach out and minister to those who are in their formative years and are ready for something to happen in their lives. They want to change the world for Jesus and are willing to get involved in that change. Reaching youth here and now should be a top priority for those in ministry, knowing their minds are still open for the gospel and willing to become disciples for the Master.

_____Chapter 3_____

ORGANIC YOUTH SYSTEM

A human body is composed of approximately one hundred trillion individual cells that work together to produce a fully functioning human body. A special symbiotic relationship exists between individual cells and the human body as a whole. One can't exist without the other. Biological cells are not independent entities that function on their own. They depend on the ecosystem of the rest of the body, and the health of the entire body draws from each individual cell. Sometimes when just a single cell becomes altered, it can dramatically change the whole body.

In the same way, individual cell groups are not independent from the rest of the body. Rather, each cell is part of a greater whole and receives nourishment from the rest of the body of Christ. When youth cells gather together in larger gatherings, the youth are encouraged by the larger group, reminded of a common vision, and receive deeper teaching.

ESSENTIAL PRINCIPLES

In most churches, youth cells are one homogeneous category among other types, which might include family cells, children's cells, men's cell, women's cells, and so forth. And even churches that began with only young people, like Dove Christian Fellowship and Antioch Community Church, eventually need to diversify as the congregation grows older.

Some cell churches have grown large enough to hire a youth pastor. The youth pastor oversees the youth cells and youth congregation, while others supervise the family cells, men's cells, and so forth. Yet most churches start with volunteer youth leaders who supervise cells and receive coaching from the lead pastor. Most cell churches emphasize the following characteristics:

- Cell
- Congregation
- Celebration
- Equipping
- Coaching
- Prayer and Missions

In later chapters, I'll cover coaching and equipping, but the focus of this chapter is defining the cell, congregation, and celebration.

CELL

The cell is a group of 3-15 people, who meet weekly outside the church building for the purpose of evangelism, community, and spiritual growth with the goal of making disciples who make disciples that results in cell multiplication.

In the following chapters, we'll explore two different types of youth cell groups. I didn't invent these categories. I acknowledged them. They simply appeared in my research.

The first type is the intergenerational cell, which involves youth gathering with adults and other age groups in the same cell. We'll explore what this type looks like, and I'll offer a few example of churches who are using them. Some churches begin with intergenerational cell groups where youth are present but eventually start youth-led cells.

The second type of cell is the student-led or youth-led cell. This is the most common type of youth cell group in my research, and the phrase "youth-led" sums up this type of group. Youth led doesn't mean that adults are completely absent. Adults often open their homes, serve as hosts, coaches, and equippers.

While the cells should remain small for relational intimacy and transparency, the gathering of those cells in a congregational service is limitless, depending on the growth of the church and the facility.

CONGREGATION

The congregation in the cell church is the grouping of specific cells into a larger gathering. If the church has women's cell groups, perhaps those women will come together for a congregational time of teaching and ministry. The same is true with men. Not all cell churches gather their homogeneous cells into congregational gatherings, but youth ministry almost always does. The youth congregation or service doesn't replace the

Sunday celebration, so youth ministry normally includes cell, congregation, and celebration.

Youth congregations might gather weekly, monthly, or only occasionally. The youth at Antioch Community Church in Waco, Texas, meet weekly in a congregational setting. The junior high students have their own congregational service and the high school students meet separately on Wednesday night. All youth are encouraged to go to the celebration service on Sunday morning.

Some youth groups will find that a monthly congregational meeting is best. Our youth ministry in Ecuador found that weekly meetings were too time consuming. We decided that the youth congregational meeting would be once per month. Youth groups start at different places. Sauder and Mohler counsel, "In a small church, you may have only enough youth to comprise one cell at first. As the group grows and multiplies, a youth celebration meeting where all youth cells come together can also be implemented."[22]

So what characterizes qualitative youth congregational gatherings? I suggest the following:

Inspiring: Synonyms for inspiring include: s*timulating, exhilarating, exciting, refreshing,* and *invigorating.* You could even use the word *fun.* Christian Schwarz writes, "People attending truly 'inspired' services typically indicate that 'going to church is fun.'"[23] Spirit-led creativity should characterize youth congregational meetings.

Sanders believes that youth need to feel like they're part of something larger than themselves. Although his goal is not to attract a crowd, he does realize that youth are drawn to larger gatherings. He said, "It's natural for young people to want to be part of something exciting."

Well-Planned: The Holy Spirit makes a service exciting, but he also welcomes diligent planning from us. The inspired spontaneity in effective youth congregational gatherings are usually the results of previous planning.

Solid teaching: the youth leader should use the congregational time to teach God's Word in a creative, interesting way. Drama is also instructive as well as testimonies of changed lives. PowerPoint can help. Teaching God's Word is foundational, but worship, drama, and testimonies should have an important role.

CELEBRATION

The celebration is when the entire church comes together in all age groups, normally on a Sunday morning. Youth and adults gather to hear God's Word. Some youth congregations have grown to the place of becoming their own celebration gathering. That is, the youth have their own "Sunday service" and do not attend the celebration of the rest of the church. When this happens, the youth no longer have a congregational event. The celebration event becomes their youth gathering.

The International Charismatic Mission is an example. The church decided to make the Saturday night youth congregation one of the five celebration services. When that happened, the youth no longer attended the Sunday worship services. The Yoido Full Gospel Church in Korea is another example of Sunday youth services. YFGC has two Sunday celebration services dedicated specifically for youth.

BEYOND YOUTH

In the 1970s we would pack my friend Rob's boxy brown van full of young people and drive twenty-five minutes down the 405 freeway to hear Greg Laurie give his weekly Monday Bible study at Calvary Chapel, Costa Mesa.

Pastor Laurie would pack out the auditorium with thousands of young people. He was funny, relevant, and spoke our language. Laurie challenged us to change the world for Jesus, and many did. Others fell away. But all, without exception, grew older. Greg Laurie himself is now sixty-four (born in 1952) and his mentor, Chuck Smith, has passed on to glory.

Having a cell system that prioritizes different age groups helps ensure that youth can gracefully transfer to become young adults, young marrieds, adults, and even elderly. In fact, more and more churches are trying to connect youth with adults from the beginning, knowing that youth ministry has a moving target. That is, youth quickly disappear into adulthood in just a moment of time.

Some churches prefer, in fact, to start with the end in mind and connect youth with adults right away. They downplay a separate youth ministry in favor of intergenerational gatherings. And certain churches have seen great fruit with their intergenerational ministry, as we'll see in the next chapter.

_____Chapter 4_____

INTERGENERATIONAL YOUTH GROUPS

When Jacob Shuey was in fourth grade, he was part of an intergenerational group (IG) at York Alliance Church (YAC). He continued with that IG group throughout his teenage years and now, nineteen years later, at age twenty-nine, he leads an IG group. "It's amazing to hear the wisdom of a sixty-year-old when you're only a teenager," he told me. "That's what intergenerational groups are all about," he said. When his family moved to York, Pennsylvania, his entire family became involved in an IG group. His dad and three younger brothers continue to be part of life groups and have stayed faithful to Jesus Christ.

IG groups are as old as the New Testament house churches because those early groups were intergenerational. They connected the parents, teenagers, children, and extended family.

The Book of Acts speaks of entire households participating in the Christian faith and describes church life happening in the believers' homes. The Bible refers to the Church as the household of God or the family of God (1 Timothy 3:15; Ephesians 2:19; Galatians 6:10).

BACK TO INTERGENERATIONAL MINISTRY

While reading the literature on youth ministry in preparation to write this book, I felt overwhelmed at times with the reams of suggestions about how to keep youth interested, attract new visitors, and run a smoothly functioning youth group. But I also noticed another thread in modern-day youth ministry that is moving away from youth as a separate entity and trying to connect youth with adults and parents.

Wayne Rice is a widely respected youth ministry trainer. For years, he conducted youth seminars and wrote dynamic youth manuals directed toward youth groups in local churches. He provided resources to invigorate youth services within the church.

Now in his later years, he advises against having a separate youth service. He now believes youth should be integrated into the adult gatherings and programs.[24] He says,

> Providing a youth service may seem harmless, even beneficial, but when we train teenagers to believe that the regular worship service of their church is inadequate both in style and content, we undermine not only the unity of the church and its traditions, but the possibility that they will ever return to the church when they grow too old for the youth group.[25]

Many of the youth experts of a bygone era are now repudiating the very youth programs they once advocated. As these youth specialists have aged, parented their own children, and then reflected back on youth ministry, they have acknowledged the inadequacy of youth events and programs to make disciples. The new trend is for youth ministers to connect youth with the adults in the church and to involve the parents more intimately in ministering to children. David Kinnaman and Aly Hawkins write:

> The concept of dividing people into various segments based on their birth years is a very modern contrivance, emerging in part from the needs of the marketplace over the last hundred years. In a misguided abdication of our prophetic calling, many churches have allowed themselves to become internally segregated by age.[26]

Intergenerational cell groups provide an important answer to connect youth with older, more mature saints and also to establish long-lasting bonds of connections. Youth and adults interact each week, and when the youth go off to college, connections are maintained. Youth have a need for elder mentors, and the adults need the vitality of the youth.

WHAT AN IG GROUP LOOKS LIKE

IG groups are like normal cells. They follow a similar order, meet in homes on a weekly basis, and last about one and one half hours. Refreshments and fellowship follow. IG cells might rotate from house to house or have one permanent one. They normally follow the 4Ws, which include Welcome, Worship, Word, and Witness. If children are present (ages 4-12), the children would stay with the entire group for Welcome and

Worship and then separate into another room for the Word and Witness time.

> **For More In-depth Teaching on the 4Ws, please see Joel Comiskey's book** *How to Lead a Great Cell Meeting So People Come Back* **(2001).**

Youth in IG groups participate with the other adults from beginning until the end. This requires that the adult leaders are sensitive to the needs of the youth, allow them to participate, and even give them special responsibilities, like leading the worship, the lesson, the prayer, and so forth. I personally think the best groups rotate responsibilities among the willing members, and youth need to fully participate in taking their turn.

Like all cell groups, the goal is to edify those present, which literally means to "to build-up or construct." Paul wrote to the Corinthian church, "What then shall we say, brothers? When you come together, everyone has a hymn, or a word of instruction, a revelation, a tongue or an interpretation. All of these must be done for the strengthening [edifying] of the church" (1 Corinthians 14:26).

The cell is the ideal atmosphere for people's lives to be reconstructed and for them to grow in the grace and knowledge of Jesus Christ. In the small group, the Holy Spirit, the Master Craftsman, challenges and changes people. The intimate atmosphere of the small group makes it possible for this edification to take place.

I recommend following the four Ws, and as time passes, more experienced leadership will learn to vary the order according to the needs of the group.

The Welcome time (15 minutes) highlights an icebreaker, which encourages people to get to know those in the group. An icebreaker question might be: What do you like to do on vacation? Or What is your favorite hobby? The idea is to connect each person in the group to everyone else.

The Worship time (20 minutes) centers on God, since the church exists to give glory to him. Whether there is an instrument or not, the goal is to acknowledge God through worship. A group can worship through singing songs, praying, reading a Psalm, or meditating on God in silence. If songs are used, it's a great idea to provide a song sheet with the songs listed for that evening (normally 3-4 songs on the sheet). Many groups use a You Tube video, worship CD, or just sing without instruments. In between the songs, the worship leader should allow group members to offer a sentence praise, prayer, or silent confession.

The Word time (40 minutes) in an IG group focuses on allowing God's Word to speak to all present, whether young or old. Cell lessons normally have about three to seven questions based on a passage of Scripture. It's a great idea for the leader to allow willing youth to take their turn in facilitating the questions, which will help the youth mature through participation.

Great leaders are facilitators who draw out others to share their thoughts and apply God's Word. They are not Bible teachers or preachers. Cell leaders should not talk too much because the goal is not information, but *transformation*. Great leaders help steer the group away from talking about world politics, criticism of the church, or the opinions of different authors. Again, the goal is to apply God's Word to daily living. People should go away changed by God's eternal message.

Members can read the Bible verses out loud. However, the leader should only ask people to read who are comfortable reading in public to avoid embarrassing anyone. It's important that the facilitator gives a brief explanation of the Bible passage—without preaching. Otherwise, members won't know how to answer the questions, not knowing the biblical context. The facilitator doesn't have to be a Bible expert to do this.

Many churches base their cell lessons on the Sunday morning preaching, and the facilitator can take notes while the pastor is preaching the message, knowing that he or she will be covering that topic during the cell meeting the following week. If the cell lesson is not connected with the sermon, the facilitator will prepare by reviewing the Bible verses before the cell meeting.

The Witness time (15 minutes) is the last part of the cell group. It focuses on reaching out to others and might include planning an evangelistic activity, preparing for some kind of social action outreach, or praying for friends and family who need Jesus.

Youth should be full participants of all aspects of the cell. Although an adult normally leads the IG group, it's possible that youth might lead the group as well. York Alliance Church is a great example of how IG groups work.

YORK ALLIANCE CHURCH AND IG CELLS

When York Alliance Church (YAC) in York, Pennsylvania, first made the transition from a program-based church to a cell church, it determined that the cells would be intergenerational.* Pastor Brian Kannel would love to say it was a wise, well-thought out decision with deep theological grounding, but that wasn't the case. Rather, there were a lot of kids, and the church needed to know what to do with them. IG groups answered that question. And in the past fifteen years, they've seen growth and maturity in the children, youth, and adults.

The church began with homogenous cell groups, but they noticed a problem. The young married couples had questions and problems that were very typical for young married couples: How do I decide on a house to buy? When should we start trying to have a family? And so, they asked others in their community. Predictably, they had no good answers. So, they pooled their ignorance and made the best decisions they could.

Meanwhile, as the group of retirees connected with one another, they discovered that while they had a lot of answers, none of them really had any questions. When they talked to one another and compared aches and pains and the current ailment of the day, they found that they didn't have the energy to even ask questions.

The church quickly discovered that IG cells were not simply a strategy to care for children. With an intentionally-integrated community, young adults had older men and women speaking wisdom into their lives. Children suddenly had multiple adopted

---

* A lot of the material in this section came from several blogs that Brian Kannel wrote on Joel Comiskey Group in May 2012: http://joelcomiskeygroup.com/blog_2/2012/05/30/our-journey-into-childrens-cells/. I've edited this material but some of the Kannel's wording is verbatim.

grandparents who loved and cared for them. The energy of young lives was somehow infused into an older generation.

Teens were no longer simply being mentored by a youth sponsor; they were being invested in by an entire family. Single men had a family to eat dinner with; widows had companionship; empty-nesters had children running through their living rooms again, which they could send back to their homes when they were ready to enjoy their hard-earned peace and quiet.

IG cells connect the best of both worlds. They bring families together to disciple children. They build up both the young and the old. Ideally, an IG cell consists of youth, children, their parents, single adults, young married couples, and senior couples or singles. However, it doesn't have to have all these ages.

TRANSITIONING TO IG YOUTH CELLS

York Alliance tried a lot of things when they first started cell ministry back in 1995. In fact, Brian Kannel, the current lead pastor, was youth pastor when they first started transitioning to cell ministry. They started with student-led cell groups using Ted Stump's material (see chapter five), but Kannel felt that the students soon began to figure out the dynamics, how to answer the questions, and eventually became less interested.

YAC tried to integrate the youth within a normal IG group along with the youth's own parents. That worked better, but there were still problems. Some youth didn't want to stay with their parents. As the leadership team wrestled with what to do, one of the leaders, Stacy Pope, said, "Why don't students attend regular cells groups where their parents are not present." It was an *aha* moment. YAC decided to clump groups of youth together into an IG group where their own parents were not present. In this way, the teens would be seen as "normal" members of the cell. YAC typically combines three or four youth together and then places them into a willing IG group. Kannel said, "Teens are herd animals and like to stay together in groups. It's difficult for a lone teen to jump into a group of adults and feel comfortable."

The goal of the IG groups at York Alliance is to treat the youth as adults. The entire process has worked well for them. They target youth in the ninth and tenth grades, and they also prepare an IG group to take on the youth. The youth step into the group on their own. It's like a rite of passage. They participate just like the adults. The youth take turns with leadership, the cell lesson, worship, icebreaker and so forth.

YOUTH HAVE A CONGREGATIONAL MEETING

YAC still has a youth congregational meeting. That is, the youth from the different IG groups meet on Wednesday night in a normal youth congregational gathering. YAC even has a youth pastor, but the youth pastor is constantly promoting the IG life groups, and understands that the primary way the youth will be cared for is in an IG group. Kannel's daughter, for example, recently brought a friend to the Sunday celebration service who had been coming to the youth ministry on Wednesday night. Kannel realizes that for this friend to really grow, she'll need to get plugged into an IG group. The youth congregational meeting provided an entry point to create interest but the IG group is where the youth are discipled. Kannel says that about fifty to sixty percent of the youth are in IG groups.

The youth congregation meets on Wednesday night and about thirty-five percent of those who attend are not in IG group. They do break up into small groups on Wednesday night, but they don't classify these break-out groups as cells. Anyone who wants to be involved in youth leadership or ministry must first be committed to attend an IG group. The youth do other activities, like retreats and outreaches, but the IG commitment is central and the main place where discipleship happens.

BENEFITS

Over the years, YAC has noticed several benefits of their IG emphasis.

First, when the teens go to life groups where their parents are not present, they are more willing to open up and share what's really on their hearts. They feel like a normal part of the cell, rather than only leading the children during the Kids' Slot.[27] Kannel said, "We have teens as young as twelve or thirteen who lead the lesson, worship, and prayer for evangelism." In other words, the youth are full participants in the cell. They grow and mature just like everyone else.

Second, the youth build relationships with other adults in the church, and adults build relationships with them. Youth receive new perspectives about adults who are not their parents.

Third, it provides a natural care structure for them when they transition into college and come home again. Kannel said, "It's exciting to see the strong bonds between the youth and their cell groups when they go off to college. Youth know people who are praying for them, and they have a spiritual family to connect with." The IG group walks with them all the way until they come back from college. While in college, they stay in the email loops, share struggles, and receive prayer. Without IG groups, the college person would often say good-bye and the connections were severed. "Now," Kannel said, "90% of returning college students to the York area reconnect with their IG cell group."

Finally, and maybe most importantly, it gives the youth a foundation for their own faith. The youth see it in terms of the Hebrew "Bar-Mitzvah," a coming-of-age event at the age of twelve or thirteen. The young person leaves the confines of their parent's group and begins his or her own faith journey. The young person learns to put words to personal conviction in the midst of a caring community.

WEAKNESSES

YAC recognizes the weaknesses of their IG groups. The major one is the lack of evangelism. They have found it difficult for youth to invite their friends into an IG environment where there are adults and children. Perhaps it's because the friends don't feel comfortable around other adults, or because it takes a while for new youth to warm up to the adults who are present.

Another limitation relates to whether the adults cell truly welcomes the herd of youth into it. If the IG group is not welcoming, the youth sense that, and it just doesn't work well. If the adults in the group don't prioritize youth, it doesn't work. The adults in the IG group need to enter into the youth's world and make the youth feel at home.

Since Kannel has become the lead pastor, there's a huge influx of children. It's not uncommon to have eight children per IG group. Those children are now becoming youth and will be encouraged to get involved in an IG group. YAC is prepared to welcome those young people into their IG groups with the hope that they will become disciples and connected into an intimate family.

IREST AND IG CELLS

iRest is an Elim Church located in Reseda, California, and connected with pastor Mario Vega and the Elim movement from El Salvador. Each year, my own ministry (Joel Comiskey Group) holds a conference at iRest and both Mario Vega and I speak on cell church topics. The participants see huge banners declaring the yearly cell goals, which happened to be 400 cell groups in 2016. From the initial cell groups in the year 2000, the church has grown to 4,000 adults and 1,500 children, with more people in cells than in celebration. iRest is an exciting cell church that is reaching the Latinos of greater Los Angeles and exemplifying the effectiveness of cell church ministry in North America.

Pastor Jorge Peña, the lead pastor, was sent to the city of Reseda, California, in 2000 with a group of family cell groups from the mother church in Los Angeles. Previously, Jorge matured in a cell group, became a co-leader, leader, multiplication leader, supervisor, network leader and then was sent as a church planter to Reseda where he began the process with a new group of people. In one year, this group of family cells had developed into a church of 300 members who were committed to reaching the city for Jesus, and the church has not stopped growing.

The unique aspect of iRest is the integration of youth and adults in the cells. iRest does not have youth cells. Rather, youth are integrated within the 380 adult cells in the church. This is a creative feature of iRest, since the Elim mother church in San Salvador does have youth-led cells, as we'll see in the following chapters.

Armando Pavón is the fulltime youth pastor at iRest. Although Armando was converted in an Elim celebration service in 2003, he was also actively involved in a cell group from the beginning. Within three months, he was leading a cell group and within two years, he had multiplied his cell four times. This is the pattern for all those in ministry in iRest, as it is in most cell churches around the world.

Like other IG cells, the youth at iRest interact with the adults, and most youth attend the cells with their parents. In fact, eighty percent of the young people between thirteen and seventeen attend the cell groups along with their parents. About fifteen percent of the youth will go with their friends to a cell group and five percent go alone to a cell group because their parents don't attend the church.

The cell groups are in Spanish, but many of the youth speak far better English. "This has been a thorny issue," Armando admitted. "We continue emphasizing Spanish because most of the adults emigrated from Latin America to Reseda and are not yet fluent in English." Although iRest has not yet started purely English-speaking cells, they might do so in the future.

Another unique aspect at iRest is that each cell has a youth representative that reports to the zone representative about the needs of the youth within that particular cell group. Each month, Pastor Armando meets with each zone representative to talk about the youth needs. They pray, plan, and visit those youth that need special attention.

Youth at iRest include anyone between thirteen and twenty-five years of age, but there are two specific categories: thirteen to seventeen and eighteen to twenty-five. Those who are between eighteen and twenty-five often lead the IG cells (approximately one hundred leaders in this category). However, this is much less common among those thirteen to seventeen. While iRest never tries to promote solely youth cells, some cells will naturally gravitate toward younger people.

All Elim churches have a weekly planning meeting and iRest also follows this pattern. The planning meetings, like the cell groups, are intergenerational. The core team, both youth and adults from each cell, meets together on Tuesdays or Wednesdays to plan for the upcoming Saturday cell. Those in the planning group are assigned things to do and ministries to cover.

The youth do come together each week for a congregational meeting. Because there are so many youth meeting throughout the Reseda area, there are four separate youth congregational gatherings of about eighty youth each week, depending on when a particular zone comes to the church for the biblical teaching.[28] Then once per month, all the youth come together for a larger congregational gathering, complete with drama and dynamic teaching. There are some 600-700 youth for these events. The youth attend one of the Sunday services, just like everyone in the church.

IG CELLS BIRTHING YOUTH CELLS

Young people often feel the inner urge to form cells with their own peers. Adults should encourage these groups and even offer assistance. One of the weaknesses of IG cells is the lack of youth participation, and this partly stems from adults not being proactive enough to include the youth in the life of the cell. Adults, like mother eagles, can help in the process by allowing the youth to launch their own cell groups. Sometimes, in fact, it's best for youth to be nudged out of the nest, so they can fly on their own and learn with their own peers.

Daphne Kirk, an expert in intergenerational ministry, encourages IG groups to nurture youth-led cell groups that are planted from the IG group. She writes, "The intergenerational cell can be pro-actively involved with the youth cell through prayer and support."[29] Kirk encourages freedom for youth to stay in the IG group, while not discouraging the formation of youth cells. When youth cells are formed, it's important to link them with the mother IG group. Adults in the IG group can play a major role in praying for the youth, hosting the group, and mentoring youth leadership.

Ralph Neighbour says something similar, "The youth cell leaders get their modeling and receive both spiritual and practical support from their intergenerational cells."[30] Both Daphne and Neighbour believe there is an important place for both youth-led cells and IG groups and that one should not exclude the other.

All adults at one time were youth and know that maturity is a lifetime process. Youth eventually will need to fight their own battles and grow spiritually on their own. Youth cells are a great way for them to exercise their gifts and talents in the presence of their contemporaries. Yet, it's very hard to do this without the support of parents and other adults. For example, adults must open their homes, drive youth to the cell, and encourage the youth to make the time to attend the youth cells.

Those planting a cell church will most likely begin with IG groups and eventually start youth cells as the church grows. The first youth cell leaders would be cared for and discipled by the IG cell group leader, becoming part of the first leadership network. The young person would be held accountable to meet with his or her coach on a regular basis. Philip Woolford, a cell church planter in Australia, planted youth cells from his intergenerational cell. He writes,

> Two homogenous cells (boys and girls) have now been established from this one adult cell. They are led by the young people, and they take pastoral responsibility themselves. The boy's cell initially met with the adults and then after Welcome/Worship left for their Word and Works time. It allows the young people to leave and establish their own cells while remaining connected to their "family cells" for support, mentoring and family ties.[31]

The connection with the IG group in the initial stages is essential in the transition. Our own church plant in Moreno Valley started with a single IG cell meeting in my house in 2003. My children participated in the IG group for the icebreaker and worship and then would go into another room during the "Word" (teaching time) for their own cell lesson. As they became older, they wanted to start their own youth cell group. My wife was instrumental in coaching second-born Nicole and then my third-born Chelsea on how to lead the cell, what material to use, and especially the debriefing times afterwards. My kids grew and matured in their own youth cells, but they were coached and supported by adults.

The youth at Dove Fellowship (founded by Larry Kreider) attended the intergenerational cells until God birthed in them the desire to start their own youth cells.[32] The adults helped in the process of youth cell formation, and the process was very organic and natural. Sauder and Sarah Mohler describe Dove's experience,

Youth cells became an informal, casual place youth could take their friends. We were careful not to imply that these youth cells were better than the adult/family cells. As they expanded, we did not require the youth to attend youth cells. They were given the freedom to go with their parents to the family cell or get involved in a youth cell, whatever met their needs best. We felt it was important that the youth felt affirmed and not forced into one pattern. Eventually, however, most of the youth got involved in the youth cells, along with some of their friends who got saved. A cell group of peers was just too exciting to pass by![33]

Dove wanted to make sure the parents were involved in the decision-making process, so they gave complete liberty for parents to either keep their teens in their IG group or to allow them to participate in the youth cells. Sauder says,

With parental consent, younger teens can join in with the youth cells already in existence. The older youth naturally mentor the young who are looking for role models. Of course, the leader of that cell and the cell members must be in favor of having his age join the cell because younger teens are less emotionally mature.[34]

In the beginning, most of the youth at Dove attended cell groups with their parents in IG groups but the problem was the lack of involvement. They often ended up sitting in cell meetings, staring at their sneakers in boredom, going out to play basketball, or taking care of the children during the cell meeting.[35]

The leadership at Dove noticed that the youth were not really growing in the IG groups. The youth needed to be prodded in order to mature. Dove Christian Fellowship decided to start two youth cells, made up of newer Christians who were not from Christian families. The two youth cells met weekly, but there were also weekly youth gathering for all the youth in a congregational setting. The experiment worked! The youth had close discipleship relationships in their cells and also continued to have the larger youth group to attend, mirroring the same strengths the adult ministry was experiencing.[36]

The label called "youth" only lasts for a short time and in a blink of an eye youth become adults. They are the "generation next," the adults of the tomorrow, the ones who will eventually lead the church. Knowing this, many churches develop the youth to lead their own cell groups, to make disciples who make other disciples. What these youth-led cell groups look like and how they are formed is the topic of the next chapter.

_____Chapter 5_____

YOUTH-LED CELL GROUPS

Ted Stump has dedicated his life to prepare students to become world-changers. Stump was considered a successful youth worker in the mid-1980s because thousands of kids were coming to Christ through his ministry. Yet, he was also increasingly frustrated by the lack of discipleship. If thousands of kids came to Christ during a three-day crusade, only a small percentage followed through with their commitment. But this was the only method Stump knew at the time. It was the typical way to reach youth back then—heavy on the flashy entertainment and low-key gospel messages and light on follow-up and nurturing. Stump saw kids having fun, but he also saw little depth fostered in them.

Then Stump heard Ralph Neighbour of Touch Outreach Ministries talking about cell groups. Neighbour said the cells never grew larger than fifteen members, they met in homes, were focused on evangelism, and were discipleship oriented. Something inside of Stump exploded. "That's the answer to the follow-up question!"[37] Soon he was studying the cell movement and ended up traveling to thirty countries where there were large, exemplary cell churches.

Stump applied what he learned to youth ministries. He trained committed student leaders to facilitate, follow-up, and nurture the groups, just like the adults in the cell church model. Stump and his ministry, Student-Led Cell Groups, have now trained thousands of youth and youth ministries in how to develop youth to lead youth cells. He has worked with some 2,000 youth ministries to help transition them to cell-group oriented youth ministry.

STUDENTS LEADING STUDENTS

In youth-led cell groups, the youth are developed to actually lead the cell groups. The host of the group is often an adult, but those leading and attending are youth. According to Stump, it's best to have a leadership team that consists of:

- student leader
- student co-leader
- adult mentor

The adults pour their lives into the student leaders by encouraging, equipping, and building them up. The adult does not lead the group but focuses on mentoring and discipling the student leaders and addressing any difficult questions and situations that may arise. Stump says, "The adult is only there to mentor, disciple and equip; they are not leading the group in any way, shape or form."[38]

Only if students step up and lead their peers will the cells reach their full potential for evangelism and discipleship. Youth have a special ability to reach other youth. While adults have to think and act like youth to reach them, youth are already there. As youth are developed and trained through cell groups, they become prepared to move into adult-led cell groups. If a student can lead a cell with peers, he or she is much better prepared for those adult years.

Students have a keen ability to reach fellow students and continue the process of multiplication. Student cell groups become the families the students never had. Yet the youth cell is not just for believers. Youth-led cell groups give students the chance to exercise their faith and to evangelize those who don't know Jesus. Lost, hurting and saved students all meet together in the cell.

First Baptist Campo Grande, located in the western state of Mato Grosso do Sul in Brazil (bordering Paraguay and Bolivia), develops young teens to lead cell groups. An adult has to be present in the teen cell group because they have found that this helps parents to release their teens to attend these groups. The adult is ultimately responsible, but the church's goal is to develop adolescents into leaders. Having an adult present assures the parents that their kids are safe and that there won't be any abuse.

Gabriel, a thirteen year old, leads an adolescent cell group. He has multiplied his cell three times since he has been in charge, although the cell itself has multiplied seven times. An adult sits in the cell with him to provide accountability. Gabriel goes to the Tuesday equipping each week, where he receives his cell lesson and training on how to teach it. Although the church gives him the lesson, Gabriel realizes he is ultimately responsible for the lesson and the life group in general, so he makes adjustments where needed. His goal is to meet the needs of those in his group.

Gabriel reaches out to his non-Christian friends at school. For example, he befriended Guillerme, who was very rebellious. Guillerme came to know Jesus, was baptized, and now his friends are coming to church. Gabriel leads the group in worship as he plays guitar. "But I don't want to do everything," he told me, "So I try to make sure that others are included in the prayers, the ice-breaker, the sharing, and other activities."

Gabriel's cell meets weekly in the same house, but it is not connected to another adult cell group. Rather, parents from First Baptist Campo Grande have opened their home for Gabriel's cell group. The church prefers to have one meeting place, so that other people will know where to go each week. It adds a certain permanency to the group.

Youth cell groups reach out to youth in the context of love, care and support. In a world that is void of meaningful relationships, kids are drawn to Christ by their peers, and in the group they can experience—often for the first time—unconditional love.

Effective youth cells meet outside the church building, with the emphasis on the home. Stump encourages the groups to meet in different homes and believes that rotation makes it easier to reach lost friends. Stump writes, "There's something special, intimate, and safe about meeting in different homes each week. Plus, it makes more sense and is easier for kids to attend meetings in homes—they're probably visiting them on a regular basis anyway."[39] It's important to create an open loving environment. Room size, lighting, chair arrangement, and how visitors are greeted contribute to the success of the cell.

The goal is to make disciples that results in multiplication. If the group has too many people, the members do not feel cared for and eventually leave the group. Adults have to give teens the responsibility of leadership while mentoring, encouraging, teaching, and yes, allowing them to fail.

NUTS AND BOLTS OF STUDENT-LED CELLS

Youth-led cell groups meet for approximately 1.5 hours. Some might stay longer, but it's important to have a start and stop time. The meeting normally includes:

- Ice-breaker. This is an open ended, interesting question that gets students talking and getting to know each other.

- Lesson. Most youth-led cell groups follow an adaptation of the pastor's message. Ted Stump, on the other hand, has developed some one hundred youth topics, which include open ended questions, discussions, testimonies, and application to the needs of youth today.[*]

- Ministry time. Students apply what they have learned during the ministry time. God's Word speaks to each person and transformation is the goal.

The best youth cells are dynamic and fun. Ice-breakers, the application of God's Word based on questions, worshipping Jesus and allowing him to speak through each person characterize great youth cells.

Over the years, Ted Stump has become increasingly convinced of the need to prioritize the Spirit's working in student-led cells. He longs to see healing take place among the students as they pray for one another. He said, "If I could do it all over again, I would spend more time equipping people in the gifts

---

[*] Ted Stump's material can be purchased at www.cellgroup.com. Telephone and email information is also available at this site.

of the Spirit. At this time in my life, I am re-thinking everything and want to emphasize worship and the gifts of the Spirit
in an ever-increasing way."[40]

Ted Stump, like many others, has become convinced that
young people need to hear and respond to the Holy Spirit in
cell ministry.

EXTENDING THE KINGDOM

John Peter began leading a cell group when he was sixteen years
old. His parents were Foursquare pastors in Belo Horizonte,
Brazil, and his group was one of the ten cell groups in the church
at the time. His involvement was more out of obedience to his
parents as the eldest child rather than a heart-felt commitment
to Jesus. Although having responsibility to lead the cell, he was
still drinking liquor with his buddies. One night he shared the
gospel in his youth cell and nine people received Jesus. As he
reflected on how God saved people through him, even though
he was not actively living the Christian life, he realized that he
had a responsibility to serve Jesus. In the process, he became a
serious follower of Jesus and gave up drinking altogether.

He began to research online about how to lead small groups
and began to apply his newfound knowledge to cell leadership.
His cell grew to sixty-six people. He knew it was too large, so
he encouraged the youth in the cell to attend IG groups with
their parents. He also started three more youth cells.

The youth eventually began to meet once per month as a congregational group, and as of 2016, the church has 380 young
people in forty-two youth cells (in a church of 600 with sixty

cells). John Peter is a fulltime youth pastor, along with three others.

Youth reaching youth through cell ministry has the potential of discipling a new generation for Jesus. Youth know their own generation and are best able to evangelize those in their own age group through meeting needs, building relationships, and establishing friendships.

Surveys have consistently shown that 75-90% of converts receive Christ because of a friend or relative.[41] So when it comes to reaching students for Jesus, it is most effective to develop a friendship with the non-Christian and eventually invite him or her to the cell. Some have called this strategy *oikos evangelism,* a strategy as old as the New Testament era, wherein *oikos* relationships were the bridge of outreach. *Oikos* is the Greek word for *house* or *extended household relationships.* In the New Testament, the gospel spread through these household and extended family relationships as the church met house to house. Applied to youth evangelism, *oikos* relationships are with those people who the youth know the best, come in contact with most frequently, and who God has placed in their path. In other words, God gives youth relationships with others, and then reaches those people through friendship evangelism.

Thayana from Belem, Brazil, developed a relationship with Elem and Edy during a homework study group time. They became friends through studying together and encouraging each other to get the best grades possible. Eventually, Thayana shared the gospel with them and asked them if they wanted to receive Jesus as their savior. They said yes and that same week went to Thayana's cell group. They felt God's love and the excitement of being part of a youth family. Everyone welcomed them and not long afterwards they went to an

"Encounter with God" retreat. God opened Elem's heart and she was baptized a couple months later. However Edy waited almost three years to be baptized. Both became powerful and great small group leaders. They are both coordinators now in the Belem ministry team.

Group evangelism is most effective when people feel comfortable. This is part of the reason why the majority of youth cells meet in homes. Brian Sauder and Sarah Mohler write, "The primary method that is used in youth groups is to have the youth cells meet in homes during the week and have a corporate youth gathering at the church facility on a regular basis."[42] Meeting in homes has the advantage of:

- Homes are more comfortable, whereas building space is more academic.

- Homes get families involved. When the student group is in the home, it gives opportunity for the adults to host the group and sometimes coach the youth leaders.

- Home groups allow more pastoral responsibility for the volunteers.

- Home groups lessen the driving distance, are more accessible to students, and allow for different meeting nights. Doug Fields, former youth minister at Saddleback Community Church, says, "The strategic positioning of our meeting places throughout the community allows us to reach more students who can't get a ride to the church property. Meeting in the homes also gives us the freedom to have alternate meeting nights and times."[43]

Apart from home meetings, some youth will meet in coffee houses, parks, office buildings, and campuses. Some of the most life-changing cell groups in the church I helped plant in

Ecuador met at universities. At one time the Republic Church had over thirty cells meeting on university campuses in Quito, Ecuador.

Some youth groups have taken the first step of transition to small groups by breaking up in smaller groups within the church after the larger youth meeting, but this should only be a transitioning step, rather than the norm or ultimate goal. The goal is to meet in groups outside the church building to penetrate a lost world. Like the early Church, youth cells take the gospel where youth live, study, and play.

RESISTANCE TO STUDENT-LED CELLS

There is a dynamic, life changing movement among teens throughout the world today. Youth cells are exploding with Holy Spirit life and fire around the world. Yet there is resistance to student-led cell groups. Two common reasons for this resistance are tradition and fear of losing control.

Tradition: Most courses or books on youth ministry fail to even mention cell groups. What is mentioned is how to attract and keep a crowd of youth in a larger congregational youth setting. Since there is an inadequate supply of literature on student-led cell groups, youth leaders tend to retreat to what they know best: speaking events and a variety of youth activities.

Fear of losing control: Most youth pastors would never overtly confess to having control issues. Yet, covertly many have imbibed the teaching that success in youth ministry depends on ministry plans and talent. Meeting in the church building simply makes it easier to control what's happening.

Knowing why there is resistance is the first step in overcoming it. Adequately equipping youth leaders and then proactively coaching the youth is the second step in overcoming resistance to student-led cell groups. There is a third step, however, that requires faith, trust, and pushing youth out of the nest, just like eagles teaching their young to fly.

HELPING YOUTH FLY

Baby eagles need a push in the process of flying—they don't instinctively fly on their own. To initiate the process, the mother eagle nudges the young out of the nest and as the eaglet falls down the face of the cliff, the mother catches and carries it back to the nest. The mother bird pushes the little one out again, and again, over and over. She never lets them hit bottom, but she does let them fall, because they have to learn something they don't know. Those little birds were made to fly, but they don't know it, so she needs to teach them. The mother eagle then pulls the nest apart because she knows the young will never learn to fly as long as they remain in the nest. Deuteronomy 32:11 says, "Like an eagle that stirs up its nest and hovers over its young, that spreads its wings to catch them and carries them aloft. The Lord alone led him; no foreign god was with him."

To help youth step out of the nest and start the process of cell leadership and ministry, it is helpful to show youth what others are doing around the world. In the next chapter we will highlight five world-changing churches that are helping youth spread their wings and fly.

Chapter 6

CHURCHES MODELING YOUTH-LED CELLS

The phrase "a picture is worth a thousand words" is a common English idiom. It refers to the notion that a complex idea can be best understood by showing an image of the idea, rather than giving an explanation. The modern day phrase dates back to 1911 when a quote appeared from newspaper editor Tess Flanders saying "Use a picture. It's worth a thousand words."[44]

When considering youth-led cell ministry, it's helpful to paint a picture of what cell churches are actually doing with youth ministry. Theory, definitions, and principles are important but practical examples help understanding by painting a picture.

The following five churches come from North and South America. There are many other great examples of youth-led cell groups around the world, but I've chosen these because

I have spent time in each of these churches and studied them in-depth. These cell churches are also well-known and have influenced many other churches and pastors to emphasize youth-led cell groups.

ELIM: FROM GANGS TO THE FAMILY OF GOD

According to UNICEF data, 38% of children and young Salvadorans live without one or both parents. The reason is mainly because of migration. Both the economic difficulties and violence have forced more and more parents to leave the country each day. Those children left in El Salvador remain under the care of other family members or neighbors, and often those children are neglected or abused.

Such conditions lead many of the children and young people to join gangs as a way to cope with their humiliating conditions. In the process, a destructive cycle is established: the greater the migration of adults, the more children join the gangs, and as the gangs are strengthened, there is more violence. And as the violence increases, there are more migrations. This cycle has turned El Salvador into the most violent country on the planet—more young people and children are killed in El Salvador than anywhere else.

Miguel grew up in this horrendous environment. Raised in a dysfunctional family, he was subject to scorn and rejection and never received affection and love from his mother who was just trying to survive. His father left the family when Miguel was two years old, moving to the United States. "My entire childhood was marked by loneliness. I went to school alone and then came back and spent time by myself. There was little food at home, so sometimes I would just go outside to forget how hungry I was," he said.

He eventually found love and acceptance with gang members who led him into sexual promiscuity and violence. "I knew that there must be something better," Miguel said. Often Miguel would sleep on the street or on the roof of his house because his mother wouldn't take care of him—even when he became seriously sick and didn't have food or medicine. One time his mother said, "Aren't you dead yet?" From that time on, he felt resigned to a life of hatred and meaninglessness.

Then a neighbor down the street greeted Miguel in a strange way by smiling at him and saying "God bless you." Miguel refused to smile back because his heart was so hard. But this young man persisted in talking to Miguel and getting to know him. He invited Miguel to a youth cell group. Out of curiosity, Miguel decided to attend.

At first it seemed strange to be surrounded with love, biblical teaching, laughter, and joy. "I felt uncomfortable because that feeling was so foreign to me, but my heart of stone began to be transformed. I received Jesus and he filled my heart with meaning and purpose."

Miguel couldn't keep this new excitement to himself. He shared the love of Jesus with everyone he knew. It wasn't long before Miguel entered the equipping track and became a cell leader. "I've now gone back to school, apologized to my mother for my hatred for her, and my life has new hope and meaning. I now live for Jesus Christ and one day hope to be a minister of the gospel."

Youth cells play a key role in providing an alternative family to broken young people. In youth cells, young people find a Christian family in which they are received with respect, tenderness, and where they have a positive place in society. Some of these young people would never go to the church building, but they have no problem attending churh in the home of another young person. They are motivated to be part of a caring community of young people who receive and accept them. Through cell ministry, many have been saved from murderous violence.

Youth cells were not always the norm at Elim. For a long time, in fact, Elim only emphasized family cells in which youth and adults mixed together. Family cells were seen as an opportunity for participation and inclusion without distinction of age. In practice, Elim was modeling intergenerational cells (IG) without even knowing there was such a concept, or if there were other options available.

Over the years, Elim decided to make youth ministry more intentional. They started a youth congregational service but soon ran out of space. Elim has six Sunday services as well as services in the main auditorium from Monday through Friday. On Saturday, the building is not used because it is "cell day," and everyone is meeting in homes throughout El Salvador. Because it wasn't possible to have a weekly youth service, Elim decided to have a once per month youth service. The results were impressive. The building filled entirely with young people eager to hear God's Word and meet other young people.

In 2006, youth cells were actually born from these celebrations. Young people perceived the need to continue growing together in multiplying cell groups. Elim began to change their supervision structure to better care for youth cell leaders and to proactively promote youth cells in their geographical districts. Elim continues to multiply youth cells while fine-tuning the equipping and coaching.

In May 2016, Elim San Salvador had 835 youth cell leaders with some 9,000 youth attending the youth cells across San Salvador. Adult cells are still the most numerous, followed by children's cells, and then youth cells. As youth cells multiply, they are giving more and more attention to the needs of the youth throughout El Salvador.

The youth leaders receive coaching through supervisors who are specifically designated for youth ministry. The youth cells, however, continue to be part of the geographical districts within the youth cell system. The coaches come from the cell system, like Armando, who at the age of nineteen became a youth cell leader and multiplied his cell various times. Eventually, he was asked to coach other cell leaders. Armando writes, "Working with young people has been a great experience for me. I'm learning as I give out, but youth teach me a lot as well. I'm growing as a disciple of Jesus as I give out to others." Serving others has taught Armando to understand God's love and care for a lost world.

All future youth leaders need to complete the normal six-month equipping, which is standard for all potential leaders at Elim. The youth also have two equipping events per year that provide additional insight into the needs of youth. In August 2010, the first youth training covered topics such as:

- Why work with youth cells?
- Qualities of youth leadership
- Organization of youth cell ministry
- Discipleship and youth counseling
- Dynamic materials in youth cells

After this training, the youth guide was first published in December 2010. The youth guide is a compilation of youth cell lessons that are used in the cell groups. The new youth emphasis reflected in the lesson guides has motivated young people who were previously apathetic to cell ministry and to the church in general.

Elim has since started weekly congregational youth gatherings, as well as maintaining a larger monthly gathering. Some IG cells were modified to become youth cells because they already had a capable youth leader. In other situations, IG groups gave birth to youth cells.

Some youth continue to attend the IG cells and are not forced to separate into youth cells. Aracely, for example, was 15 when his grandfather took him to an IG cell. Attending the IG cell with his grandfather changed his life. He found warmth, love, acceptance, and a new family to share with. Throughout the process, God began to heal Aracely from the myriad of resentments he felt toward his parents and his general situation in life. As he focused his attention on others and their needs, his life began to change.

Aracely was baptized, began attending the Sunday celebration service at Elim, went through the cell leaders training, and eventually became a youth cell leader. So in Aracely's situation, the IG group gave birth to his own youth cell.

ANTIOCH: STUDENTS TRANSFORMING STUDENTS

Antioch Community Church (ACC) in Waco, Texas, has been a long-time advocate of youth-led cell groups. Blake Foster, the youth pastor in Waco, Texas, says "Life groups help disciple our youth. They get into the lives of the youth with the gospel message." Foster realizes that it might be more convenient to only meet in a larger congregational group, but youth need up-close personal attention.

Foster oversees some 150 high school students meeting at
different homes throughout the Waco area. Approximately
twenty to thirty high schoolers meet in each home, but the
larger group is then broken down into smaller "D-groups."
The larger cell group meets for forty-five minutes, and then
the smaller *D-groups* (2-3 per group), meet in different places at
the same house, either inside or outside for the next forty-five
minutes. The D-groups are gender specific, so boys meet with
boys and girls with girls. They try to combine more mature
youth with less mature ones. The following is covered in the
two 45 minute periods:

45 minutes all together

- 10 minutes of mingling
- 15 minutes of a game or engaging activity (get people laughing and comfortable)
- 5 minutes of sharing the vision of why small groups are important as well as any announcements
- 15 minutes of worship (2-3 songs)

45 minutes in discipleship groups

Weekly Check-In and Follow-Up

- How was your time with God this week?)
- How did you do in the area of sexual/emotional purity?
- Did you follow through with what we talked about last week?

Word time

- Prayer for God to speak through the Word
- Scripture reading, preferably in two different versions
- Application of God's Word
- Summary of passage

Prayer

- Intercession for each person present
- Prayer for God to give specific insight to each person
- Prayer for any specific needs in the group

The high school students at ACC do meet together as a congregation on Wednesday night. The junior high students have their own cell groups and congregational service as well.

Joel Sanders, youth pastor at All Peoples Church in San Diego, was part of the original church planting team sent from Waco to plant All Peoples Church. The youth were already meeting in a congregational meeting on Sunday night when Sanders began leading the youth, so he started the weekly home groups, following the biblical pattern of Acts chapter two. The youth also gather with the rest of the church on Sunday morning.

Sanders asks senior high schoolers to lead the youth cells because they are more mature. Sanders pours into the leaders, knowing that coaching is essential to make the groups work. "There is a new life and dynamic through the home groups," he said. They've seen healing among the youth. One girl, now a life group leader, had a suicide planned out with a date and a place. The members of the life group ministered to her, and she realized she should not go through with it. God's love and care broke through and she now sees life from a totally different perspective.

One life group planned an outreach in a high school that was mourning the death of a student. Life group members offered to pray for those in grief, ministering to those who were hurting. Various high schoolers received Jesus. One female cell member saw an inappropriate Facebook post from another cell member. After getting counsel from those in cell leadership, she talked to the person even though it was a hard step to take. The person not only received her counsel but also repented and asked for prayer.

Sanders said, "More than anything I have seen the youth become disciples and develop as leaders." Life groups at All Peoples Church (and Antioch in general) invite Jesus to speak through them and in them. Many have been encouraged as they share what God is doing in their lives. Activities covered in High School Groups at All Peoples Church include:

High School Groups at All Peoples Church

- Icebreaker: something fun, often with food, get to know each other time
- Vision casting and announcements
- Worship. Allowing the Holy Spirit to move through the gifts of Spirit
- Bible Discussion: Application of Sunday evening youth lesson
- Ministry/prayer time

BELEM FOURSQUARE: RADICALS FOR THE LAST GENERATION

Pastor Valter, third generation in a family of Foursquare pastors, grew up in the church. At the age of twelve, Valter was playing drums on the worship team, growing in Christ, and looking for opportunities to serve Jesus. He and his brother started a youth cell that multiplied to four groups in 2001. By 2007 the youth cells had multiplied to forty cells and Valter became the youth pastor in his father's church. Valter attracted the attention of Josué Bengtson, apostle and founding pastor of one of the largest Foursquare churches in the country in Belem, Pará Brazil. Josué Bengston extended an invitation for Valter to join the church staff.

When Valter first started at the Belem Foursquare, the church leadership team was just learning about cell ministry. As a pastoral team, they visited cell churches and held a training once per week. There were about twenty youth in the church at that time. Since then the youth cell ministry has grown to 450 youth cells and 2,700 people attending the weekly youth service on Sunday night (an official celebration service of the church). They have approximately 3,500 participants in cells during the week.

The youth cells outnumber the adult cells in the church and the church's example has helped propel the entire Brazilian Foursquare denomination to make the transition to cell-based ministry. Encouraged by youth ministry in Belem, many Foursquare churches have revitalized their youth ministry.

Valter and team call themselves Radicals of the Last Generation, which turned ten years old in 2016. The vision is associated with the ministry of Aimee Semple McPherson, the founder of the Foursquare, "conquer the lost at any cost." The youth live in a radical way, willing to live for the dream of making Christ known. In fact, the youth live like it was the last generation and a sense of urgency has taken hold of their hearts.

Their daily life is intense. The young people live for Jesus not only in the cell meetings but on a daily basis as described in book of Acts. The cells have a planning meeting every week to pray and think about what they will do in every cell encounter and, above all, to invite Jesus to be the center and the leader of every activity.

They have a prayer room, open from Tuesday to Friday, which is called the Azusa room, named after the great Azusa Street revival. In daily shifts, the youth go there to cultivate time with God. They believe that revival is their destiny and are preparing to see Jesus accomplish signs and wonders in their midst. They believe that the entire city can be saved. The senior pastor and apostle, Josué Bengtson, says that those who do not want to be saved will have to move out. Of course, he's joking but this is the zeal that pervades the church.

The youth baptize people every three months. All cells pray and work for the sake of bringing at least one person to salvation and water baptism. They have an equipping school called Radical Growth Line, in which the young people can feed their faith and grow in the Christian life. They study topics like worship life, signs and wonders, history of revivals, and grace.

Every year, Radicals of the Last Generation hold a conference for youth throughout Brazil. In 2016, the theme was "Reactivating the Supernatural." They emphasize God's supernatural reality and his desire to work today like he did in the book of Acts. The doctrine of the Foursquare in Brazil is that Jesus not only baptizes with the Holy Spirit but promises that the outpouring is available for all who believe (Joel 2:28).

Ninety percent of the cells are led by youth, but some adults are also involved in the leadership. Intergenerational cells are not common in the church because most youth do not come from Christian homes. The youth cell order is similar to other youth cells:

- Icebreaker
- Worship
- Word or lesson time: All groups follow the same lesson. The youth ministry provides material for the youth cells, which is planned for the entire year. Each lesson follows the biblical teaching the youth are following throughout the year.
- Prayer and outreach

One of biggest struggles is the lack of consistency among youth. Youth get enthusiastic for a while but the excitement may fade. Some leaders fall away, so the Belem Church is constantly equipping new youth leaders and diligently coaching the existing ones. Another struggle is sexual promiscuity. Some youth don't want to wait for the right God-given person, choosing rather to have sex without getting married. These issues often come up in the regular encounter retreats and ongoing equipping. Even though there are struggles, Jesus continues to transform lives and make disciples at Belem Foursquare Church.

THE VINE: CHILDREN BECOMING YOUTH LEADERS

The Vine Church in Brazil has been actively developing children in home cell groups since 1999. They now have 10,000 children's cell groups worldwide with some 100,000 children participating. The Vine Church lives with the future in view, knowing that the present children will soon be in their early teens and become part of youth ministry. The preparation is not complete unless children enter youth ministry.

When a child reaches the age of thirteen they graduate to a youth cell, and later to an adult cell. The Vine has a special ceremony for those graduating from the children's ministry, and they carefully shepherd the graduates into youth cells. Since the children only know the atmosphere of the cell and celebration, they are like fish in water—it's the only environment they have experienced. Young teens are ready and eager to get involved with other youth and continue the process of discipleship. Testimonies abound of children who were born again in a children's cell group, discipled in the process, and are now preparing to be pastors and church planters.

The Vine believes that children and youth are best prepared to become disciples in the home environment, just like adults. They also realize that they will never reach the multitude by requiring the children to come to the church building. Rather, the Vine takes their cells to the neighborhoods.

Pastor Naor is the main youth pastor at the mother church in Goiana where there are 1,600 youth cell groups with 15,000 youth attending. There are now 7,000 Vine youth cells throughout Brazil and once per year the youth cells come together to celebrate what God is doing.

Vinicius Motta, one of the network youth pastors under pastor Naor, is twenty-four years old and supervises sixty youth cells in the mother church. Vinicius was four years old when his father became sick with cancer. Through this terrible experience, God saved and discipled the entire family in one of the Vine cell groups. Vinicius attended the children's cell and received Jesus when he was six and one-half years old.

God gave Vinicius a hunger to read the Bible and at the age of twelve, he felt called to lead a cell. As part of his preparation, he went through an Encounter retreat. At the age of thirteen he started a cell group of teenagers in his house.[45]

Leading a cell group was a great experience for Vinicius. He became more responsible and mature in the process of leading others. He evangelized his friends and made disciples, thinking to himself, "I can have disciples, just like my father; these people can live the same life that I live." He multiplied his cell three times in the first year, and then multiplied it each year for the following four years. Eventually he became a coach of other leaders and then a pastor.

Vinicius said, "It was difficult growing up because I spent so much time in ministry and people would say, 'You are so young. Why don't you have more fun and live like normal people.'" Yet at a young age, he learned what it was like to live for Jesus and deny himself. Vinicius is now married and looking forward to starting a family. He said, "I love to see 40,000 young people come together each year in the local soccer stadium to give glory to God." In this annual rally, the Vine casts the vision for youth cells conquering the world for Jesus. Many youth cell leaders are becoming pastors, and now the youth are sending out their own missionaries.

The Vine youth cell groups are for those thirteen to twenty-six years old. In the mother church, there are some 400 teen cells, which includes those between thirteen and nineteen. They have another grouping of twenty to twenty-five years olds. The youth cell category is mainly non-married people, although some married couples do volunteer to help with the teen cells. But for the most part, once a teen marries, they become part of the married cells.

All of the youth cells meet weekly in homes, but more recently they have decided to open cell groups on university campuses.

Sometimes they have an adult present, but not all the time. The order for the youth cell is:

- Icebreaker (15 minutes). The goal is to get to know each other and have fun.
- Worship (30 minutes). Worship songs and prayer for one another. Invitation for the Holy Spirit to move in their midst.
- Word (30 minutes). This is not a preaching time. Rather, the cell leader stimulates everyone to talk. The goal of the cell is to apply God's Word and transform lives in the process.
- Witness time (15 minutes).
- Eating together.

Youth cells start with about seven youth and multiply when there are fifteen participants. The norm is to have between eight to nine youth per cell group. The youth also have their own congregational gatherings during the week. They call themselves the Free Radicals because they desire to live a radical lifestyle for Jesus and change the world in the process.

ICM: FROM DRUGS TO YOUTH CELLS

I visited Bogota every year for five years (1996-2000) to learn more about the amazing youth movement at the International Charismatic Mission (ICM). During those five years I got to know César Fajardo, the leader of the original youth movement at ICM. Fajardo did most of the creative, balanced thinking in those early days of the Groups of Twelve Movement. I have the greatest respect and admiration for César Fajardo and know that he never intended Groups of Twelve to become so

divisive in many circles around the world.[46] In 2004 Fajardo
left ICM to open his own church called Church without Walls.

As the original youth pastor at ICM, Fajardo successfully
transformed a ragtag group of young people into an army
of 18,000 youth meeting in 8,000 youth cells and celebrating
in their own youth service on Saturday night. When Fajardo
started the youth ministry at ICM in 1987, there were thirty
young people attending. He began to dream of reaching the
lost youth of Bogota. When he preached, he imagined that the
place was filled. He openly declared to his small group, "There
will come a time when young people will have to line-up to
enter this church." In 1987, Fajardo took a photograph of
the nearby indoor stadium full of people. He then hung that
photograph on the wall in his room and began to dream and
believe God to fill it with young people.[47]

Approximately 500 youth receive Christ during each Saturday
night service. I could never sit in the service without weeping,
knowing that God was transforming drug addicts and gang
members through the multiplying youth cells. The youth vision
is contagious. Visiting pastors caught it. One pastor wrote,

> The atmosphere was electric with the Holy Spirit—to
> watch these young people worship with such fervor
> and pray with such intensity was a deeply moving
> experience, and I found myself weeping throughout
> the service. This meeting is a giant reaping machine as
> we discovered in all of their services. The preaching
> was hot and straight—Youth Pastor César Fajardo
> spoke on tearing down the lies of the devil. At the
> end of his ministry four to six hundred young peo-
> ple responded for salvation. The converts were then
> escorted (led by a man carrying a flag) to another hall
> through streets lined with people waiting for the next

meeting who applauded them. Once in that hall they were preached to, registered and followed-up.[48]

Pastor Fajardo passed on his vision to those on his team. Vision runs deep at ICM. It's contagious. Disciple-makers develop easily in this atmosphere, but the vision begins at the top.

Daniel is an example of God's transforming power. He first attended ICM in 1995 and accepted Jesus at a Saturday night young people's service. Jesus saved him from a life of drugs and worldly dealings. Soon after receiving Jesus Christ, he attended an Encounter retreat, School of Leadership, second Encounter, and then opened his cell group. I witnessed one of his cells that was meeting in the open air. "Is that a cell group?" I asked. The group seemed strange since it was meeting outside the indoor stadium. "Yes, this is one of our open cell groups to reach people for Jesus," Daniel told me. Daniel's network grew to thirty-five cells and eventually Daniel became a fulltime employee at ICM, working for the radio station.

I met another 18-year-old student with 380 youth cells under her supervision. Each week she attends a leadership cell in addition to leading her own leadership and evangelistic cells. She practices three days a week as a youth worship team dancer. She ministers in the Saturday evening youth service and teaches in the School of Leaders on Sunday morning.[49]

Freddy Rodriguez, a key part of the youth ministry grew a network of 1,500 cells. Before 1987, Freddy lacked hope and confidence. His life centered on drugs and alcohol. His family had separated and his father, who lived in the United States, wanted nothing to do with him. In this state of loneliness and frustration, Freddy received Jesus at ICM in 1987 and became one of the twelve disciples of César Fajardo. At that time there were only sixty people in the young people's group.

Before leaving with Fajardo to start Church without Walls, Freddy led the worship on Saturday night for over 18,000 young people. He would meet weekly with César Fajardo, his discipler. From talking with Freddy over the years and observing his life, I noticed that Freddy is totally sold out to Jesus Christ and understands that only Christ can grant success. Freddy lives in close communion with Jesus and teaches his disciples that they must maintain intimacy with Jesus at all costs. Freddy expects his disciples to pray diligently, fast regularly, and engage in spiritual warfare. God himself has given Freddy a vision for multiplication and discipleship.

It's quite easy to start youth cells for a couple weeks or months. It's a lot harder to sustain them over the long haul. The churches in this chapter have continued to multiply youth leaders and youth cells year after year. They have a built an infrastructure of youth cell ministry, which includes the building blocks of coaching and equipping. They send out youth leaders who are properly trained, and then they watch over those leaders through intimate coaching to ensure their success. In the following chapters we'll take an in-depth look at equipping and coaching in youth ministry.

_____Chapter 7_____

EQUIPPING TOMORROW'S
LEADERS

As many as 250,000 boys under the age of eighteen served in the British Army during World War I.[50] Many were gripped by patriotic fervor, sought escape from grim conditions at home, or just wanted adventure. Technically the boys had to be nineteen to fight but that didn't stop a multitude of four-teen-year-olds and upwards from joining the army in droves. They responded to the Army's desperate need for troops, and recruiting sergeants welcomed them.

World War II was no different. Many of those drafted in the U.S. were eighteen and nineteen. One soldier writes,

> When I was eighteen years old I was drafted into the United States Army. I was then trained as a medic. One of those duties was to care for the wounded. I

was nineteen years old when I crossed the Atlantic in October 1944 on the Queen Mary. This was the average age of the American infantry, between eighteen and twenty years old.[51]

It is one thing to send a young person to battle; it is quite another to prepare the youth to fight well. Effectiveness depends on the training. The soldier's boot camp experience was invaluable. Over and over the surviving soldiers talked about how much they hated, yet needed, the boot camp training. In actual battle, they would respond subconsciously to what they learned through the repeated boot camp drills. The monotonous workouts they loathed during boot camp saved their lives by helping them to respond efficiently and automatically in the battle.

Young people, along with all believers, are on the front lines of spiritual warfare, whether they like it or not. Satan and his demons want to destroy youth today. To defeat the enemy and live victoriously, youth need to draw on biblical truths that come from deep discipleship equipping. I'm referring to the essentials of the Christian life: how to pray and read the Bible, submit to the Lordship of Christ, overcome spiritual darkness, have a daily quiet time, and how to share the gospel message.

I like the term "discipleship equipping," because it speaks of making disciples who make disciples. Effective youth ministries develop the youth through discipleship equipping that prepares them for the battle, just as boot camp prepares a soldier for battle.

Youth discipleship equipping develops the new Christian from conversion to forming part of a cell team. However, this will only happen when church leadership realizes that equipping new disciple-makers is the chief task and that establishing a strong discipleship equipping system is a top priority.

EQUIPPING TEAMS OF LEADERS

The New Testament writers avoid the idea of one leader. The norm for those early house churches was to have a team of leaders, rather than just one. Team ministry strengthens youth ministry and provides added relief, both for those who oversee or coach the youth, as well as for individual youth cell leaders.

Not everyone should be the point person in the cell, but everyone can be part of a core discipleship team. Jesus himself had a core team consisting of Peter, James, and John (Mark 5:37). Those indivdiuals who still need to develop character qualities can be part of a discipleship team without being the point leader of the youth cell.

It's liberating to future leaders when told that they will not be leading the group individually but will function in a team. Potential leaders feel more secure when knowing they won't have to do everything themselves. New groups are also much healthier when led by a leadership team. Ideally, all team members will have completed the discipleship equipping.

How many should be on a cell team? Jesus had a team of three from among the twelve, but a team might also be larger, as is exemplified in the missionary team of Paul the apostle (Acts 12:25; 13:1; 15:39). But a team might also be smaller. Jesus sent his disciples in groups of two to start home groups. Scripture says, "After this the Lord appointed seventy-two others and sent them two by two ahead of him to every town and place where he was about to go. When you enter a house, first say, 'Peace to this house'"(Luke 10:1-5).

I believe it's best to have one person guide the leadership team at the small group level and church level. Even with the emphasis of plurality of New Testament leadership, there are indications that a point person led the house church teams (e.g., 1 Timothy 5:17). When no one is in in charge, it's common for no one to take responsibility, which leads to lack of clarity and direction.

Team leadership functions should be distributed according to the giftedness of each member. If Joe has the gift of evangelism, he should be responsible to organize the small group outreach. If Nancy has the gift of mercy, she can help in the visitation of a hospitalized member or organize the visitation. If Jose has the gift of teaching, he can rotate in leading the small group lesson or in the taking a member through the church approved training. If Jeanie has the gift of apostleship, she should be spearheading the next multiplication. If Andrew has the gift of administration, he can be in charge of distributing small group responsibilities—who brings refreshments, leads worship, prayer, lesson, and so forth.[52]

Once you've established who will be on the team, emphasize love and servanthood. Team members should talk directly to other team members, rather than gossiping—especially avoiding the subtle trap of gossiping in the name of praying for so and so. Absolute honesty and willing to walk through conflict—and actually growing through it—are important traits that make or break effective team ministry. Remember that even the great apostle Paul couldn't handle one of his own team members and ended up leaving his team due to conflict (Acts 15:2). Team ministry can be intense, and therefore it's essential to have a forgiving spirit, allow love to cover a multitude of sins, and especially to develop friendship among team members. In fact, friendship is the glue that sustains the team over time.

I'm convinced that team leadership is essential for effective cell ministry. Yes, there's a price to pay with shared leadership and most likely conflicts will occur. However, the rewards and fruitfulness of team leadership far outweighs the difficulties along the way. Team leadership also paves the way for fruitful, healthy cells that don't depend on one person. As Solomon once said long ago, "Though one may be overpowered, two can defend themselves. A cord of three strands is not quickly broken" (Ecclesiastes 4:12).

LOOKING FOR FAST YOUTH

Youth are dreamers and often live in an ideal world. Many youth fail to match intention with reality. Some need more time to mature. While all youth should be equipped, some youth tend to be more reliable as cell leaders and team members. A great acrostic to evaluate this is called FAST: Faithful, Available, Servant-oriented, Teachable.

Faithful: A person might be exceedingly fruitful, but if he or she is not faithful, that person can't be trusted. A large part of fruitful ministry is just showing up, being there on time, and possessing a quality of responsibility—people can count on the person to fulfill what he or she says. Long-term ministry requires faithfulness. It's one the critical aspects of leadership.

Available: A young person's availability demonstrates priority. In other words, people make time for those things which are important. When a young person is willing to hang out a little longer, clean-up when everyone is gone, and volunteer for ministry assignments, it's usually a sign that youth ministry is important. Doug Fields writes about how he picks his potential leaders,

> Who's doing the jobs that other students believe are beneath them: picking up trash, stacking chairs, and cleaning up . . . , I hope to see students reaching out to the unconnected or shy students, the ones in the corners who keep their distance from the crowd. And when everything appears to be done, I look around to see who has stayed behind looking for an opportunity to help with anything. It's easy to slip out the door and miss seeing a few students offering to work when everyone is tired. These three groups of students provide relief and give me ideas for potential leaders[53]

Servant-oriented: what kind of attitude does the potential leader have? If the young person is gruff, uncaring, and even rude, that person is not ready to be the point person on a leadership team. Jesus prioritized the humble servant task of washing the feet of his disciples and warned against lording over others. Possessing knowledge is far less important than applying biblical truths in a way that models the discipleship principles Jesus left with his disciples. And one of the most important discipleship truths is love and servanthood. Having a servant-heart is an essential trait in ministry.

Teachable: Completing the discipleship equipping is a good place to start, but there's always more to learn in life. Discipleship never reaches the completion point in this life. Does the potential leader act like he or she has arrived? It's very hard to coach someone who resists counsel and suggestions. Most of the deep lessons are learned along the way, in the nitty-gritty moments of life. If the youth pastor or coach can't approach the potential leader to offer corrections, future ministry will break down and rebellion might occur. It's best not to give leadership positions to those who are not willing to learn and willingly receive correction.

Beyond FAST, transparency and maturity are important traits to look for in potential youth leaders. Transparency can definitely be modeled and taught, whereas maturity comes over time with experience. Because maturity takes time, often youth workers look for cell leaders who are slightly older than those they are leading. Brian Sauder writes,

> It is probably a good idea for the youth cell leaders to be at least one level of maturity ahead of the people in their group. For example, senior highers lead junior high cells, and if they have the maturity, their senior high peers. Without this maturity, it can prove to be too much of a burden for a senior higher to lead his peers, even with close spiritual covering by youth leaders.[54]

YOUTH EQUIPPING STEPS

To win the next generation, equipping is essential. Discipleship equipping turns members into ministers and gives them confidence to open their homes and penetrate the non-Christian community for Jesus Christ.

The best equipping in youth cell ministry involves personal interaction between leader and disciples. Personal attention is critical.

Equipping needs to be *doable* with regard to time and *flexible* with regard to options in taking it. Flexibility happens when the youth understand the goal: making disciples who make disciples. Discipleship equipping should not be complicated but clear and simple. The average time frame to complete it is from four to nine months. Many cell churches have advanced discipleship equipping for those who complete the first level. Six key principles are vital to effective discipleship with youth.

Joel Comiskey's book, *Leadership Explosion* (2001), details the principles how cell churches around the world equip their people to become disciple-makers. Comiskey's book *Making Disciples in the Twenty-first Century Church* (2013) highlights how making disciples is the essence of cell ministry.

PRINCIPLE #1: KEEP THE DISCIPLESHIP EQUIPPING SIMPLE

The attention span of youth is short. It's important not to have too many steps in the first level, making the discipleship equipping long and cumbersome. Potential youth leaders might never arrive at the point of being part of a discipleship team in a youth cell.

Don't over complicate the initial discipleship equipping that makes disciples of new believers and prepares them to reach out to friends and neighbors through cell ministry. Most cell church equipping tracks prepare their leaders in the following areas:

- basic doctrine
- freedom from bondage (Encounter retreat)
- personal devotions/quiet time
- personal evangelism
- leadership training

PRINCIPLE #2: PROVIDE ACTION STEPS WITH THE TRAINING

The best training is accompanied with practical, on-the-job experience. The potential leader needs to see and experience community life, especially evangelism. I encourage the following action steps:

- First step: learn foundational truths of the Christian life. Action step: get baptized.

- Second step: attend an Encounter retreat. Action step: break from sinful habits.

- Third step: learn how to have a quiet time. Action step: have a daily quiet time.

- Fourth step: learn how to evangelize. Action step: sharing the gospel with a person with whom you have developed a relationship.

- Fifth step: learn how to lead a cell group. Action step: become part of a discipleship team or the point person leading a youth cell group.

Remember that youth should practice what they hear in the equipping. They will not only want to hear about evangelism (third step) but should go out and evangelize.

This is also true in leading a cell group. The youth taking the equipping will need to practically experience what they're learning, so it's best if they are actively participating in their own cell group.

Pastor Jim Corley developed his own step-by-step process that is both clear and concise:

- Join a cell group.

- Complete the course *Crossfire* (offered during Sunday school, in a Saturday seminar, or before/after cell). Action step: Get baptized and become a member.

- Attend an Encounter retreat. Action step: Break sinful habits.

- Complete the course *How to Have a Quiet Time* (offered during Sunday school, in a Saturday seminar, or before/after cell). Action steps: Practice regular personal devotions, be assigned an accountability partner by the cell leader, agree to serve as an apprentice cell leader, complete the spiritual life assessment.

- Complete the course, *How to Evangelize* (offered during Sunday school, in a Saturday seminar, or before/after cell). Action step: Share testimony with a non-believer and give a gospel presentation.

- Complete the course *How to Lead a Cell Group* (offered during Sunday school, in a Saturday seminar, or before/after cell). Action step: participate in each aspect of cell leadership with the goal of being involved in a new cell launch, either as a team member or point leader.

PRINCIPLE #3: ACKNOWLEDGE VARIETY IN METHODOLOGY

The equipping can be taught in a variety of ways. Don't confuse the methodology (where or how youth are trained) with the discipleship equipping.

I've noticed a great variety of methodologies for implementing the training. It's possible to teach the discipleship equipping before the youth service, during the Sunday school hour, or individually. You can do it before the cell starts, after the cell finishes, or during a day-long training.

The discipleship equipping can take place in a variety of places. Many churches use their Sunday school hour for the equipping within the church building. Others like to use the home environment. Others ask cell members to complete the discipleship equipping on their own and then might meet one-on-one in a Starbucks, McDonalds, or any place conducive for communication.

PRINCIPLE #4: USE ONLY ONE EQUIPPING TRACK

Though flexibility should be allowed in the choice of when and where to equip people, I counsel churches to have only one discipleship equipping—although that one discipleship equipping should be adapted for the youth.

Many pastors hesitate in implementing a discipleship equipping because they're not sure which discipleship equipping is the best or what material to use. If the pastor is not the creative type, it's best to use someone else's discipleship equipping material in the beginning. The goal, however, is always to adjust and adapt until the discipleship equipping is one hundred percent part of the local church culture.

I don't think it's necessary to create a separate youth discipleship equipping. Rather, I counsel youth workers to adapt the adult equipping to make it more dynamic and relevant for youth, while maintaining the basic essence of the adult equipping. This ensures that the entire church is learning similar doctrines and disciplines of the Christian faith.

Jose Abaroa, youth minister at Cypress Creek Church (CCC), encourages all youth to take the church-wide equipping which begins with a spiritual formation weekend called an Encounter retreat. They try to have two Encounter retreats per semester. They also have additional steps to the equipping after the Encounter and one of those steps is prayer equipping—how to pray both personally and as a group. Cypress Creek breathes the life of prayer, mainly because Cecilia Belvin, pastor of prayer at CCC, has developed one of the most vital prayer ministries I have ever witnessed in a church.

The Vine Church in Brazil has one equipping for all those leading cell groups, whether adult cells, youth cells, or children's cells. As youth go through the equipping, the same material will be applied differently to the youth, with illustrations that reflect youth culture. Yet, the teaching is the same.

The first step in the Vine Church is an Encounter retreat. In the mother church in Goiania there is an Encounter every weekend. The Encounter starts on a Friday and ends on Sunday. People are saved, set free from sin, healed, and filled with the Spirit. On Sunday, people testify of how God has changed their lives. Then the person goes through the rest of the equipping. They call it the Winner's Path. The steps are:

1. Encounter retreat
2. Living Waters course
3. Baptism
4. Discipleship course
5. Spiritual Maturity course
6. Leaders Training course

All those in the church are encouraged to take the entire equipping, and finishing the equipping is a requirement for leadership. The Vine has a mission to develop an army of leaders who can change the world, starting with the children, then the youth, and continuing in the adult years.

First Baptist Campo Grande (FBCG), located in Campo Grande, Brazil, equips the adolescent cell leaders on Tuesday night with topics like:

- Biblical foundations
- Caring for one another
- Leading people to Jesus
- Cell group essentials
- Phases of the cell group
- Leadership dynamics
- Discipleship
- Group multiplication
- Supervision

FBCG also teaches the adolescent leaders on how to lead the weekly lesson.

Belem Foursquare in Belem, Brazil, features a one year equipping that includes:

- Baptism
- Encounter with God
- Personal seven-week discipleship after the Encounter retreat

- Weekly training. This training never stops. There is training for new believers and older believers as well. In those weekly meetings, they have a course called *Let's Go*, which is geared toward preparing future youth cell leaders.

PRINCIPLE #5: EQUIP EVERYONE TO BECOME A DISCIPLE WHO MAKES DISCIPLES

Ideally, each new believer should immediately start attending a cell and begin the equipping track. In reality, it often takes more time. However, the more a church closes the gap between idealism and realism, the more effective it will be. The goal is to make disciples who make disciples and this includes everyone. Not everyone will become the point person on a leadership team but everyone can be part of a leadership team.

For many years, I proclaimed that everyone should be trained to become a cell leader. Yet, I came to realize that the Bible didn't directly say that everyone should become a leader. Jesus himself used the word disciple to describe his followers. God began to change me and help me to grasp a more biblical basis for the essence of cell ministry, which is to make disciples who make disciples. This should be the goal of the equipping and the reality is that everyone can be part of a team of disciples who lead a cell group.

PRINCIPLE #6: CONTINUALLY ADJUST AND IMPROVE THE TRAINING

My advice is to adapt, adjust, and improve the training system as feedback comes in from those who have taken it. You won't have an amazing equipping immediately. Even if you use someone else's equipping, at first it will feel like Saul's armor on David. It won't be your equipping. This is especially true in youth ministry. You'll need to adjust the equipping to make it relevant for youth today. But the good news is that God loves to grant the power of creativity to those who ask, and he'll show you how to make the equipping your own.

Discipleship equipping is essential in the preparation of youth leaders and discipleship teams. Yet, it's possible to equip a person and even a team, only to see the group fizzle out over time. Often the reason for failure has nothing to do with the discipleship equipping. The problem lies in follow-up; it's a coaching issue. Leaders and teams need a coach for them to stay healthy over the long-haul—especially after birthing new cells and disciples.

Chapter 8
COACHING YOUTH CELLS

I live in California, and like most places in North America, I'm totally dependent on a car to get around. Public transportation is simply not adequate to drive me to the store, airport, or to a home group during the week. In some places, like Manhattan, New York, however, the subway and train system is far better than a car due to traffic congestion and lack of parking. Transportation depends on a number of factors, like context and technology.

The transportation of the early nineteenth century was the horse and carriage. It wasn't until the end of that century that railways changed people's lives and habits. But even after the advent of the railway, remote areas still relied on the horse for local transport. Horse-drawn stagecoaches helped people get from one place to another.

The word coach originally came from an old Hungarian term referring to the carriages and carts that were made in the village of the Kocs. On the American western frontier, the large four-wheeled horse-drawn carriages were also called "stagecoaches." The use of the term evolved in the nineteenth century as a part of university slang to mean an instructor or trainer, "the notion being that the student was conveyed through the exam by the tutor as if he were riding in a carriage."[55]

Coaches are those who carry leaders from one place to the next. They don't simply teach; they carry and come alongside. The word *coach* is descriptive of the role a person plays as he or she supports cell facilitators under his or her care. It is not a sacred term. In fact, churches use many terms to identify the role played by the cell group coach: supervisor, section leader, G12 leader, cell overseer, cell sponsor, even *L* (which is the Roman numeral for *50*). I've written extensively in other books about the different coaching structures that cell churches use.*

The main coach in the cell church is the lead pastor, who coaches leaders in a variety of age groups. Youth cells comprise one network in the cell church vision. The lead pastor is the main visionary and shepherds the youth worker who in turn cares for the youth cell leaders. Granted, there are churches that are led by youth pastors over a youthful congregation, but eventually, like in the case of Dove Christian Fellowship,

---

* In my book, *Passion and Persistence: How the Elim Church's Cell Groups Pene-trated an Entire City for Jesus* (Houston, TX: Touch Publications), I talk about Elim's coaching structure, how their coaches are organized, what each level of coach does, the schedules, and how coaches are developed. I have two books on the G12 structure: *Groups of Twelve* (Houston, TX: Touch Publications, 1999) and *From Twelve to Three* (Houston, TX: Touch Publications, 2002). These book explain how G12 groups are organized and how they can be adapted.

the youth leaders grow older, have children, and eventually are looking for leaders to disciple the youth. Coaching is critical to ensure that leaders are successful over a long-period of time.

DEVELOPING COACHES FROM THE CELLS

Those coaching youth cell leaders should come from the cell system. That is, the coaches should first have been developed in a cell group, led a cell, multiplied it, and supervised those multiplication leaders.

We've met pastor Valter from Belem church in earlier chapters. Although pastor Valter is the lead youth pastor, Belem church has developed ten other fulltime youth pastors from within. Each one of these youth pastors was developed in the youth cell system. Each one first led a cell, multiplied it, and then coached the new leaders. God's calling and Christian character played an essential role, but these pastors also experienced cell ministry firsthand and have greater knowledge and authority in their current roles.

When a church transitions to cell church ministry from a traditional church, it takes more time to develop coaches from within. One church decided to transition to the cell church but had already hired a youth pastor to run events and programs in the traditional format. The lead pastor wanted counsel about how to integrate this youth pastor in the cell vision. I encouraged the pastor to ask the youth pastor to lead a cell, multiply it, and then coach a network of youth cells. I counseled against allowing this youth pastor to do his own thing, run his own programs, and not be integrated into the cell system.

Mario is a coach at the Elim church. At eighteen years old, he met his wife in a youth cell, although he didn't know they would marry at the time. Yet, his attraction for her was a primary motivation to attend the youth cell. As he listened to the Word of God and interacted with others, he was transformed by God's Word. He was able to transparently talk about his hurt, wounds, and abuse and found God's healing. He went through the six-month equipping, multiplied his cell group more than once, and eventually became a coach of youth cell leaders.

SPAN OF CARE

The number of cell group leaders a coach should oversee varies from church to church, depending upon the vision of the church and the capacity of the coach. If the coach also leads a small group, I would say that the coach should not take on more than three leaders. If the coach doesn't lead a small group, five is acceptable. When coaches care for more than five leaders, the coaching quality often suffers.

I encourage leaders of mother cells to coach the leaders of daughter cells from their own group, if the leader of the mother cell is willing and has the time. The reason is because a relationship already exists between mother and daughter leaders. Like a mother caring for her children, the leader of the mother cell has a special affinity for the new leader and will most likely take greater care in visiting, praying, and ensuring the leader's success.

Sometimes the mother leader is not able to coach the leader of the daughter cell because of time constraints, desire, or coaching ability. In these cases, it's best to assign a coach to the new team leader. The key is that each new leader has a coach who is praying, visiting, and serving the leader.

The Belem Foursquare Church picks supervisors from those who are already leading groups, but eventually the leader will stop leading the group and focus more on the coaching. The supervisor gets the reports each week and reports on what is happening to the leadership team. The leadership team at Belem chooses the coaches based on character, maturity in Jesus, and fruit in cell ministry.

SPENDING TIME WITH LEADERS

Personal time between coach and leader is the glue that keeps effective cell ministry from falling apart.

The lead pastor coaches the network leaders (including the youth point person); the network leaders coach the cell leaders who in turn pastor the members.

Jose Abaroa, youth pastor at Cypress Creek Church has developed strands, which work alongside the youth cells. The strands meet every two weeks, while the youth cell groups meet weekly. A leader of a youth cell must be in a strand to receive coaching.

I recommend at least once per month coaching meetings in a group context (the coach with all of those leaders he or she is coaching) and once per month one-on-one between leader and coach. The group context brings out common problems and encourages the leaders to interact with one another. Individual coaching helps the coach meet the deep personal needs with each leader (e.g., family, personal needs, job, and spiritual life).

Youth ministers (paid or volunteer) should spend the majority of the time coaching the leaders or supervisors, depending on the size of the youth group. The best youth ministers coach

the leaders and then allow the leaders to pastor the members
in the groups. The ineffective youth ministers bypass the cell
leaders and attempt to pastor the students directly.

Some leaders need to meet more frequently than two times
per month. Other leaders need less time. Jim Egli, who did his
Ph.D. on cell ministry, writes,

> Coaches need a personal meeting with their small
> group director or pastor at least monthly. Small
> group leaders need two connections with their coach
> each month—one that focuses on ministry to them
> personally and one that focuses on the mission of
> their group. At bare minimum coaches should meet
> with their leaders at least once a month. The big
> advantage of meeting twice a month or every other
> week is that it enables you to move beyond personal
> ministry to your small group leaders to actual planning
> and problem-solving.[56]

Doug Fields, talking to youth pastors, says,

> Because of the high requirements for student leaders,
> there should be a high reward. Student leaders should
> get more time with you and other adult leaders. I
> make no apologies that I spend most of my student
> time with student leaders. I do visit students at their
> games and on their campuses, but I almost always go
> with a student leader. I want to spend my time being
> a leader of leaders.[57]

COACHING KEYS

Effective coaches hone in on the specific needs of the leaders. What is the leader lacking? What particular needs does the leader have? To do this effectively, certain coaching principles are important.

PRAYER

Coaches go to battle on behalf of the leaders under their care and provide spiritual protection against Satan's onslaughts. Effective coaches cover the leaders with a prayer shield and then when they talk personally, there is a unity that has already been developed through prayer.[58] I encourage coaches to pray continually for their leaders, and then tell them about those prayers. This will help tremendously in the spiritual realm and give the leaders renewed hope and confidence in ministry.

LISTENING

The most important element of effective coaching is listening. Often the leader already knows what to do. Coaches can get so focused on what they want to say that they forget that the real work is listening. The coach needs to recognize that his or her agenda is secondary to the leader's agenda. A great coach knows when to shut up and let the other person speak.

Preparing to listen requires some pre-meeting homework. Such preparation involves thinking about each leader's circumstances and needs. It's a great idea to write down notes and insights about the leader that can be reviewed before the next meeting. This helps the coach remember past conversations and prepares the coach to listen more intently.

Great coaches don't just listen to what has taken place in the cell but are also concerned about the leader's life in general—emotional struggles, devotional life, and work. Often there are burdens that need to be shared in order for the leader to do a better job. The coach draws the leader out through careful listening.

ENCOURAGEMENT

Encouragement is critical because small group team leaders often don't feel like they are doing a great job. They compare themselves with others and feel like failures. They hear about the other team leader who already multiplied the cell and won multiple people to Jesus. "Why aren't more people coming to my cell group?" Effective coaches use every opportunity to encourage the leader. "Jim, you show up for every cell group. Great job. That takes a lot of effort because I know you are busy."

CARING

The pastor cares for the coach and the coach cares for the leaders. The leader in turn cares for the members. Everyone needs to be coached and cared for. Coaching helps the system to flow together—just like the early Church. Often the best way to care for the leader is to be a friend. The phrase "friendship with a purpose" sums up what coaching is all about. Jesus, the ultimate coach, revealed this simple principle in John 15:15 when he said to his disciples, "I no longer call you servants, because a servant does not know his master's business. Instead, I have called you friends, for everything that I learned from my Father I have made known to you."

DEVELOPING

Coaches develop the leaders in both formal and informal ways. A coach supports each leader's ministry by connecting him to necessary resources, such as curriculum, equipping, or prayer support. A coach might say, "John, here's a link to an article about listening. Please check it out and we'll go over this next time we meet." Or if John is not the type that would go to the Internet to check it out, the coach would simply print it out and give it to the leader. Later the coach would ask the leader what he or she thought. If the leader is not willing to commit to doing it on his or her own, it might be a good idea to read the entire article with the leader.

PLANNING

Coaches help the cell leader envision future disciple-makers by encouraging the leader to develop strategic planning to get everyone participating in the group. The coach might say, "Tony, have you noticed Jill in your group? Why don't you consider her as a future leader?"

The coach also reminds the cell leader that strategic planning should include encouraging all members to take the discipleship equipping, knowing that no one will be a future team member without graduating from the equipping process. Effective coaches also help in the birthing process as the group sends out a new team of leaders.

CHALLENGING

When a team leader is stagnant, the members feel it. They wonder what's wrong with the group. Vitality is lacking, the lesson is unprepared, and the leader exudes a certain dullness.

Effective cell coaches are close enough to detect the leader's lifelessness. The coach must be willing to speak directly to the leader, knowing that the leader's negative spiritual condition will affect those in the group. Paul, in his message to the Ephesian house church, said, "Instead, speaking the truth in love, we will in all things grow up into him who is the head, that is, Christ" (Ephesians 4:15).

Great coaches seek to model Paul's words by honest interaction and asking the hard questions. I encourage coaches to start with the phrase, "Can I have permission to share something with you?" The leader should know that the coach will give a straight answer and not beat around the bush.

CELL VISITATION

One of the foundational ways of coaching is visiting the cell leader's group. In this way the coach can see what's really happening—not just what the leader says is taking place. When the coach does visit the cell, I encourage him or her to blend in as one of the cell members and to participate like any other member in the cell group.

Visiting a cell group is one of the best ways for the coach to observe cell leader patterns. Does the team leader talk too much? Not enough? How does the leader deal with the talkers? The silent ones? Did he or she follow the cell lesson plan? End on time?

When talking with the leader personally about the cell, start with positive aspects and then highlight areas that need to improve. This will help in the discipleship process and encourage the leader to grow closer to Jesus.

TEAM COACHING

Youth pastors must be in step with the lead pastor's vision. Hopefully, the lead pastor is passionate about cell ministry and guiding the youth minister down the same path. Foster said, "Youth ministry is very hard. One reason is that the youth pastor has to be 100% in step with the lead pastor's vision. Without this complete submission to authority, it's easy to fall into a *me against them* mentality."

The youth minister should constantly remember that the lead pastor is human and will make mistakes, just like everyone else. Perfection is in the realm of angels, not humans. The lead pastor will forget birthdays, compliments, and commitments. Youth workers need to give the pastor grace to not be perfect. The sooner the youth worker realizes this, the better.

TAKE THE NEXT STEP

Pastors and leaders can sometimes feel overwhelmed when it comes to prioritizing youth ministry. But it's important to remember that the first step doesn't have to be a big one. My advice to pastors and leaders is to start small. I remind them that they don't—and won't—have everything figured out when they start. But it's far more serious to fail to try. The next chapter will articulate a series of steps, with the goal of making the transition to youth in cell ministry.

Chapter 9

TRANSITIONING TO YOUTH CELLS

Somebody said, "The good thing about being young is that you are not experienced enough to know you cannot possibly do the things you are doing."[59] Youth are open to experiment with new challenges and don't mind the change it brings. Change, new directions, and flexibility sets young people apart from others. They are not afraid of the twists and turns that lie along life's road. They expect them. In fact, life quickly becomes boring for youth when schedules and plans become too rigid. And maybe this willingness to change is why God often reveals his plan to the youth before the rest of the church catches on.

Long-term success in transition to youth cell ministry requires a deep conviction and commitment to the values behind making disciples in cells. But the transition doesn't stop there.

It must go from the vision stage to the planning stage to actual implementation.

Check out Comiskey's book, *Myths and Truths of the Cell Church* (2011) to learn about pitfalls to avoid when transitioning to cell church ministry

STEP 1: ARTICULATE THE VISION

When starting youth cells, it's best to highlight those values and priorities that will guide the teaching and strategies over the long-haul. Starting youth cell groups just because someone else is doing it won't sustain youth ministry when the difficulties come. And they will come. But they can also be overcome when there's a deep set of convictions that youth cell ministry is the right way to go.

The conviction that youth are disciples who can make other disciples is the bedrock foundation for starting youth cells. Too many churches don't take youth seriously until they become adults. When a church passionately grasps that youth best become disciples through cell ministry, the church will do what it takes to develop a youth cell system.

The pastoral team needs to take the necessary time to pray and formulate the values and principles for starting youth cells. The youth worker must clearly communicate the vision and the transition, both to the pastor and the youth. This means entering into sincere, meaningful relationships with potential student leaders and adults. As the pastoral team determines the values, these convictions will help the church to know how to invest time, energy, and resources for the youth.

All too often youth workers make the mistake of being lone rangers—and eventually feel isolated and neglected. Effective youth workers get the church leadership's blessing and minister within a team environment.

Lead pastors have the responsibility of launching and maintaining the vision for the church. And this vision must include youth. If the youth worker feels like he or she is always walking on egg-shells, it will be very difficult to go forward. The lead pastor needs to know that developing youth is a long-term commitment that must continue beyond the pastor's tenure. In fact, today's youth will replace the current pastor someday.

Transition is not an easy road, and churches should prepare for it. A vision for youth cell groups requires an entirely different attitude toward youth. Not counting the cost and taking the necessary steps to ensure success will result in stagnation and even future resistance. Yet many churches have successfully launched youth cells and made them a vital part of the church. The difference between success and failure in transition to youth cell groups is preparation, prayer, and persistence.

STEP 2: PREPARE THE PARENTS AND CHURCH

The place to start in helping parents embrace youth ministry is sharing biblical truths, presenting the motivation for developing youth cells, and emphasizing how both the youth and parents will benefit as a result of this new integration.

Point the parents back to New Testament house-to-house ministry, in which the churches were in the home, and youth played a vital part. Home cell ministry provides far more opportunity for youth living out their faith, as youth are integrated into the life of the "real" church. They will see their parents actively participating in worship, fellowship, communion, and application of the Word—not as spectators but as active participants.

Some will resist, thinking that the only way to minister to youth is through programs and teaching on Sunday. The reality is that youth in cell ministry enhances the Sunday teaching by application of the church teaching in the weekly cell groups, where youth can ask questions and interact with the teaching. Youth will experience what it means to be brought up within the context of a family. Faith is embraced through quality relationships—not quality programs.

Prepare the parents to be hospitable. In practical terms, this means teaching parents about placing people before things, making disciples of youth ahead of clean carpets, and viewing the home as a place of ministry rather than a private castle. The reality is that house-to-house New Testament ministry will require sacrifice. Working with youth in homes also requires an ongoing discussion between the parents and church.

It is wise to remind parents that youth are adaptable and will love the change. The adults are the ones who need to check their view on including youth in their church life. Parents should be helping their youth make the adjustments, but the whole group must participate in a new, changed attitude toward youth. The good news is that the adults will see and hear some wonderful things from the kids.[60]

STEP 3: UNDERSTAND THE PROCESS OF CHANGE

Managing the dynamics of change is one of the most important issues leadership will face in starting or rebuilding the youth ministry. People need time to process ideas. Their heads will nod with enthusiasm when hearing about prioritizing the youth in small groups, but often they haven't considered the implications. Give people time to process the new ideas as you carefully explain how the changes will benefit their families.

The well-worn adage applies to youth ministry: "Everything takes longer than you expect; even when you expect it to take longer than you expect."

In fact, any time something new is introduced into the life of the church, there is the potential for conflict. Once an organization or system gets in motion, it tends to keep going in the same direction. People become comfortable with their traditions and patterns. Everyone likes something new—for a little while. But when push comes to shove, they'll reach for the old, the established, and the traditional. This is human nature.

People might get excited about transitioning to youth cell groups, but when it involves their commitment, like taking youth to the cells, it is easy to revert back to old patterns of ministry. I like to use the phrase "programmatic knee jerks" to describe what takes place after the initial changes. Suddenly people begin to realize that the change will affect them in the practical details of daily living. It might affect the normal youth programming, requiring opening their homes for youth cells, or driving youth to their activities.

Allow for several years to transition youth into cell ministry. I know of one youth worker who failed two years in a row to establish youth cells. But he didn't give up, and in the third year, things changed for the better. It takes time for new groups to start, existing ones to crystalize, and coaching and equipping to start working properly. Persistence is often the main factor in achieving success and avoiding failure.

STEP 4: START WITH A PILOT GROUP

It is important to start the first cell with youth who are spiritually strong and emotionally healthy. Why? Because it's important to start off with a successful cell rather than a potential failure.

The trials will come soon enough, but initial short term victories will have a positive and lasting psychological effect.

The dictionary defines a prototype as, "An original type, form, or instance that serves as a model on which later stages are based or judged." In the early stage of the transition, it is important that other members can see a successful cell which can be an inspiration for others to follow.

Starting a pilot group proclaims that youth cell ministry is better "caught than taught." Rather than starting the transition by "teaching" the youth about this new approach, it best to first allow them to "experience" youth cell ministry. Those initial leaders will then impart to others what they experienced in the initial group.

Mistakes made in the prototype stage are more easily corrected before they are allowed to spread throughout a large group of cells. Key leaders are part of the process from the beginning, making it more likely they will continue to actively support youth cell ministry. Even Jesus started by forming his own prototype cell. He spent years developing the model. He couldn't afford failure. Sauder and Mohler write,

> This kind of model cell group should be made up of those who have already committed to be youth cell leaders and others who are potential leaders. In this clear model, you can train and help your leaders to see what a cell is and how it functions. The model should include an outward focus with evangelistic efforts.[61]

After a certain period, the pilot cell multiplies into the first youth cells. How long before this happens? I would recommend between four to nine months. Sauder and Mohler write,

Your youth cells will resemble what you model in the prototype cell. Make the quality of this cell a top priority because it will be reproduced over and over. This clear modeling will help your youth cell leaders keep from returning to old "Bible study" paradigms or drifting back to the way things used to be.[62]

It is always best to start new groups in at least a team of two participants. So if there are twelve in the pilot group, perhaps the pilot group could give birth to three or four new youth cells.

If the church decides to do IG cells, the process of integrating the youth will flow more naturally within the overall cell system, since youth will simply be part of the IG pilot group. If the church is just beginning cell ministry, the first IG cell should be led by the lead pastor of the church. If the church already has cell groups but is just beginning to integrate youth into the IG groups, it's best to pick a healthy adult cell and then include youth within that cell. Short-term victories are important to encourage other adult cells to also invite youth to join.

As cells continue to multiply, the traditional youth organization leadership (e.g., president, elected officials) can be transformed into a ministerial team of youth cell leaders. The youth pastor or key youth leader should ask those who have multiplied their cells to meet regularly with him to plan, pray and give oversight to the rest of the youth.

STEP 5: ADJUST AND PERFECT

A church never arrives at perfection. It simply continues to perfect what is already there. There is always room for improvement, such as fine-tuning the dynamics of the group, the discipleship equipping, and perfecting the coaching of youth cell leaders.

The moment, in fact, that a church thinks it has arrived, it probably has already begun its downward spiral. John P. Kotter, business professor at Harvard University, wrote a book called *Leading Change*, in which he talks about complacency being the enemy of progress.[63] Professor Kotter's advice is to practice gut-level honesty and to avoid a sense of complacency at all costs.

The Vine Church has excelled in their cell structure partly because they have developed a first class coaching structure for all youth cell leaders. Each youth cell leader has a coach who meets with the leader each week. Perfecting their coaching structure has taken a long time with many revisions being implemented along the way.

The discipleship equipping is another area that needs to be fine-tuned. Perhaps the church will use the one it already has, adapting it to meet the needs of youth. Carefully select and equip student leaders. Pray for start-up leaders and train future leaders through the discipleship equipping. Remember, growth cannot be achieved beyond your ability to produce new leaders.

Another area that needs to be constantly evaluated and improved is the recruitment of new workers for teaching youth in the larger gatherings and the cells. New workers are always needed to open new groups and to replace the ones that stop. Recognition of those ministering to youth is an area that is frequently overlooked. Most churches need to improve in this area. And even though the leader knows his or her reward is in heaven, God tells us to appreciate those who labor among us (1 Thessalonians 5:12, 13).

TRANSITIONING AS A CHURCH

When transitioning to youth cells, it's ideal if the entire church is transitioning to cells at the same time. Brian Sauder and Sarah Mohler, youth leaders of Dove Christian Fellowship's cell groups, wrote about how Dove transitioned their youth ministry,

> Though it is not absolutely necessary, it is actually best if the whole church is transitioning to cell groups at the same time, not just the youth group. It will be helpful because the parents will also be getting teaching from the Word and hearing vision for cells at the same time as the youth. This will make it easier for the parents to understand and embrace the vision for their teen's involvement in part of the fresh, new vision.[64]

Transitioning an entire church means that the lead pastor and team must first catch the vision. Prayer and promotion (pre-transition) are essential in making a successful transition.

DON'T WAIT

Don't wait for perfection before starting your youth cell ministry. Granted, you need to spend enough time to digest the values and biblical foundation behind cell ministry, but then it is best to get started and perfect the process as you move along. You'll adapt as you press ahead. God will give you insight as you prepare youth through cell ministry. He's more interested than you are in discipling youth to reach a lost world for Jesus.

_____Chapter 10_____

STARTING YOUTH CHURCHES

When Jesus saw the incredible needs around him and especially those who were helpless and harassed and in need of a
shepherd, he said to his disciples, "The harvest is plentiful but
the workers are few. Ask the Lord of the harvest, therefore,
to send out workers into his harvest field" (Matthew 9:37-38).
We've seen how youth can lead cells and multiply them. But
what about church planting? As I travel around the world, I
passionately plead with larger cell churches to hear God's call
for missionary church planting. But why not start this vision
among youth?

Mark Senter III, youth professor at Trinity Seminary in
Deerfield, Illinois, and one of the leading researchers on
youth ministry today, believes that youth ministry finds its
full potential when youth are sent out to plant new churches.
He writes, "Perhaps the answer to the problems created by
discontinuities in discipling relationships lies in a new vision

of youth ministries: Youth pastors should become spiritual midwives and assist in birthing new churches."[65] Senter describes more specifically how youth would be involved in planting new churches,

> Youth staff and students evangelized and discipled through the youth ministry would become the nucleus of the new church. The families of the students and former students under the youth minister's care would be encouraged to participate with their children in the project. Though the idea has some inherent weaknesses, most of them could be minimized by careful selection of the youth minister, along with a mentoring relationship with the senior pastor. The concept would require a paradigm shift both on the part of church and within the youth ministry fraternity.[66]

Senter's vision is significant because of his experience and expertise in youth ministry. Senter has dedicated his life to youth over a lifetime and has concluded that youth church planting is the best possible scenario for youth ministry.

Paul the apostle was the most effective missionary church planter of the first century. He planted simple, reproducible churches and moved on to spread the gospel. He could say, "So from Jerusalem all the way around to Illyricum, I have fully proclaimed the gospel of Christ" (Romans 15:19). Before AD 47 there were no churches in these provinces. In AD 57 Paul spoke of his work being accomplished.

In the cell church movement worldwide, there is a renewed interest in planting smaller, more reproducible cell churches. Very few cell churches grow to megachurch size. Most are nimble and simple. The best church planters are those who have multiplied cell groups and supervised the new leaders. They possess the vital, needed experience to plant a church.

To better understand church planting, see Joel Comiskey's book *Planting Churches that Reproduce* (2008)

Jimmy Seibert saw wonderful fruit with student-led cells in Waco, Texas, on the Baylor campus. God created a youth movement on campus of some 600 students in sixty youth cells. Eventually the Antioch church movement was formed, which has its main church building close to the Baylor Campus in Waco, Texas. Seibert writes,

> Our goal in college ministry is to see students transformed by the power of Jesus Christ, brought into belong in his body and released to fulfill his wonderful purposes in the world. To achieve this end we have arrived at a very simple and effective formula. It is: Cell Groups + prayer = world missions.[67]

The Antioch church plants around the world often start their churches near college campuses because the focus is to raise up a new generation for Jesus who are willing to reach their world and plant new churches. Seibert writes, "The vision and purpose of cells is to win souls for the Kingdom of God, as well as pastor one another. Though some cell meetings focus more on evangelism or edification, each cell gathering must encompass a vision for both."[68]

In 2008, Antioch Church in Waco, Texas, planted All Peoples Church in San Diego, California, with the vision of reaching young people and promoting missions. Lead pastor and founder, Robert Herber, moved from Waco, Texas, with a team of people, and among that group was Joel Sanders, who is now the youth pastor. The All Peoples Church has grown into a church of over 1,300, but they have not forgotten their church planting roots. All Peoples Church holds annual church planting and mission conferences and has planted churches in Thailand and Mexico with plans for church plants in South Africa and Moldova in 2017.

The Antioch Community Church (ACC) movement has never been content to grow one church larger and larger. Yet as the mother church gives itself away, it has continued to grow over the years. Like the New Testament Church, God has called them to become a church planting movement. Some of these multiplication pastors will plant churches nearby. Others will become cross-cultural missionaries to plant cell churches on distant shores.

Dove Christian Fellowship (DCG) is another worldwide church planting movement that was born out of youth reaching youth in cell ministry. Church planting is at the heart of Dove, and as of 2016, there were 388 Dove churches worldwide in twenty nations and five continents. Dove encourages young people to plant simple, reproducing cell churches and house church networks.

In 2011, I gave a church planting seminar at the Vine Church in Goiana, Brazil. Joseph, a young person, told me that he began his journey in a children's cell but now was planting youth based churches. He simply continued to multiply leaders and the Vine trained him during each stage of the process. The Vine Church, in fact, encourages everyone to consider becoming a church planter. Character and fruitfulness are key characteristics but cell ministry is the perfect schooling or preparation for those who want to continue the process of making disciples through church planning.

Pastor Valter at Belem Foursquare is encouraging youth to consider church planting. He and his leadership team are becoming a sending church and planting cell churches around the country and world. The lead pastor, Josué, is constantly talking about opening new churches and the youth are a key part of this. The youth love a challenge and pastor Valter instills them with the vision of sending groups of youth cells to plant new churches all over the world.

Asia is another place where youth are challenged to plant churches. Ben Wong, founder of Grace Church in Hong Kong, has dedicated his life to plant reproducible cell churches around the world. Young people are the cornerstone in making this happen. Ben wasn't content with simply growing his own church larger and larger. He developed a resource sharing network called The Cell Church Missions Network (CCMN), which is primarily concerned with mobilizing cell church people to finish the Great Commission.

CCMN hosts a youth cell church mission network during the same time period each year to challenge youth to plant churches. They believe that those who have led and multiplied a cell group are the best missionaries to penetrate the unreached cultures because they've already experienced fruitful ministry in their own culture. CCMN has sent out some 175 missionaries between 1997 and the present and held over one hundred mission conferences. CCMN missionaries are on thirteen fields, including, Macau, China, Japan, Thailand, Bangladesh, India, Cambodia, Indonesia, the Philippines, Pakistan, Turkey, North Africa, and the Middle East.[69]

I have no doubt that youth planting youth churches will become a significant force in the twenty-first century Church. Youth desire to change the world and have a God-size vision to fulfill that dream. Church plants need new people, new ideas, and new vision if they are going to emerge out of the darkness into the sunlight. Youth have what it takes to make this happen.

Established churches tend to be more concerned about building upkeep, the personality of the new preacher, who's on the board, and the program schedule for the upcoming year.

Church planting requires both vision and effort. Church plants are completely stripped of all illusions. The process is one of do or die. Reach out or close the doors. Invite or implode. Church planters are desperate for growth. Without growth, the church folds. This reality keeps church planters on their knees, crying out to God.

Unless church plants organize around evangelism, no one will show up. After all, most Christians would rather worship in a full-service church where their needs are met. Few modern-day Christians with families are willing to join a new church where programmed ministries don't exist. Christian Schwarz in *Natural Church Development* reveals that church plants are more effective in every area (leading people to become Christ-followers, baptizing members, and ministering to needs). He writes:

> If instead of a single church with 2,856 in worship we had 56 churches, each with 51 worshippers, these churches would, statistically win 1,792 new people within five years—16 times the number the megachurch would win. Thus we can conclude that the evangelistic effectiveness of minichurches is statistically 1,600 percent greater than that of megachurches![70]

Struggling to start a church does wonders for youth church planters. They are developed and honed in the crucible of church planting.

Whether church planting or transitioning, those ministering to youth are on the cutting edge of ministry. They are the ones preparing the next generation, and need to stay healthy and connected to the Vine, Jesus Christ. The next chapter highlights some bedrock truths for staying healthy over the long haul.

_____Chapter 11_____

YOUTH LEADER ESSENTIALS

Paul commissioned his hand-picked mentor, Timothy, to lead the famous Ephesus church. But by the time of the book of Revelation (approximately 90 AD), this once great church had largely forgotten Jesus in their busyness to perform. They were more caught up with doing rather than being. Their good works were numerous, but Jesus had to graciously remind them of something far more important than what they could offer. They needed to return to their first love (Revelation 2).

Busyness before being is a common problem and a trap that anyone can fall into. Christ's friend, Martha, had to learn this lesson. She entreated Jesus to badger her sister Mary to help with the busy work. Jesus turned to her and said, "Martha, Martha, you are worried and upset about many things, but only one thing is needed. Mary has chosen what is better, and it will not be taken away from her" (Luke 10:38-42).

While this chapter is primarily written to those overseeing youth ministry (e.g., pastors and coaches), the following principles equally apply to cell leaders, team leaders, and those who volunteer to reach youth today. Those who minister to youth first need to seek Jesus and make sure they are fresh and in tune with God. Youth worker, Jon Ireland, confesses his own dryness in youth ministry:

> Lately, my passion for ministry had diminished. My love for the students was lost somewhere along the way. I had become increasingly frustrated by the lack of spiritual growth in our students as well as the lack of commitment from our volunteers. I was working harder than ever, yet I felt less appreciated than ever. In addition to all this, I secretly felt that I was worth a lot more money than what I was getting paid. Mysteriously and tragically missing in my life and ministry was Christ. Dependence on Jesus had disappeared somewhere along the way. Serving God has replaced seeking God. Running a program had replaced representing the "Person."[70]

I appreciate Ireland's honesty because running a program, rather than ministering from the abundance of Christ's life, can happen to anyone. We've already seen how the church of Ephesus fell into the routine of good works, eventually becoming dry and barren.

PRIORITIZE PERSONAL TIME WITH GOD

Having a daily quiet time helps the youth leader know God, feed from his Word, and be empowered by his Spirit. In the quiet time, a weary youth minister worships the King of kings, listens to his voice, and receives direction for each day.

Experienced youth pastor, Mike Yaconelli, says, "It sounds scandalous, self-centered, and selfish to suggest that your time alone with Jesus is more important than time alone with students, but if we are responsible for our own souls first, time with God is important."[72]

Prioritizing Jesus daily will help the youth leader grow accustomed to his voice. That same voice will give the leader words of counsel while ministering to others. As he confesses and surrenders weakness to Jesus, there will be new power and guidance to minister to others. Romans 15:13 says, "May the God of hope fill you with all joy and peace as you trust in him, so that you may overflow with hope by the power of the Holy Spirit." Youth workers need God's joy and peace to be effective minister to others.

I'm convinced that the quiet time is the most important spiritual discipline in the Christian life. Doug Fields in his book, *The Purpose Driven Youth Ministry*, talks about how he personally was broken through youth ministry and learned to depend on God through the failures.[73] He writes,

> Instead of trying to please others, I have learned to live my life for an audience of One. Doing God's work isn't as important as being God's person. Since I tend to be a people-pleaser, I need a continual reminder that God is more concerned about my spiritual health than about my youth ministry hype.[74]

The quiet time provides the youth worker with a daily checkup and a time to express cares and concerns to the Creator. It is where those ministering to others receive joy and peace that will overflow to others. It is the opportunity to talk directly with the One who deeply loves and cares and chose his children before the creation of the universe.

HOLINESS

A 2016 study of pastors and youth pastors commissioned by the ministry of Josh McDowell revealed that many pastors struggle with pornography. The study included 432 pastors and 338 youth pastors and showed that "Most pastors (57%) and youth pastors (64%) admit they have struggled with porn, either currently or in the past." But the more shocking finding was, "Overall, 21 percent of youth pastors and 14 percent of pastors admit they currently struggle with using porn."[75]

Sexual temptation is a common problem among youth workers. Sexual sin happens so suddenly, but in reality it's not sudden at all. It happens over time. It's the little slip of integrity, the quick glance at porn, or the text with sexual innuendos that should never have been sent. The old saying is true, "Sow a thought; reap an action; sow an action; reap a habit; sow a habit, reap a character; sow a character, reap a destiny."

D.L. Moody once commented, "Character is what you are in the dark." God works on the leader's character because he knows that character will eventually determine long-term effectiveness. Most of the requirements in the New Testament, in fact, involve character. Virtues such as honesty, faithfulness, and good judgment are synonymous with New Testament leadership. No amount of talent or giftedness can replace these characteristics. Bad character qualities will ultimately show up, while good ones will shine over the long haul. Repentance, prayer, and accountability help youth workers to avoid sexual sins.

REST

I like to get things done. That's the way God made me. Yet, several years ago when I was planning how I could do more, the Lord convicted me to stop "doing." God reminded me that I was more important to him than what I accomplished. He wanted me to rest.

God made the human body to run effectively for only six days out of the week—not seven. Genesis 2:2-3 declares, "By the seventh day God had finished the work he had been doing; so on the seventh day he rested from all his work. And God blessed the seventh day and made it holy, because on it he rested from all the work of creating that he had done."

God's truth about resting applies to everyone, including youth. When the youth leader exemplifies taking one day off per week, he models what he wants others to follow. Resting one day per week will also make the youth leader more effective because he or she will have more to give the remainder of the week.

I talked to one pastor who refused to take a day off because he insisted that those who he was counseling needed him too much. He felt it would be sinful to neglect the dysfunctional people who needed him. He couldn't imagine selfishly thinking of himself and not being available 24/7 for those who needed his counsel. "But you're not going to help them," I told him, "if you're frazzled and burnt out." He didn't accept my counsel. I learned the sad truth that he died two years after our conversation. I have no idea why or how he died. I do know he was close to burn out when I talked with him and that he refused to consider resting one day per week.

I don't believe that we need to rest on one specific day (e.g., Saturday or Sunday). Youth ministers often have their busiest schedules on Saturday or Sundays, so it's best to choose another day. Regardless of the day, the goal is to fully rest, refraining from work.

The 24-hour day of rest should not have a lot of rules and regulations (e.g., can't do this, can't do that, etc.). You will need to do some work, like washing the dishes and taking out the trash. But as much as possible try to avoid the regular, job-related work that you do the other six days of the week. Leviticus 23:7-8 says, "On the first day hold a sacred assembly and do no regular work. For seven days present an offering made to the Lord by fire. And on the seventh day hold a sacred assembly and do no regular work." The emphasis is on "regular work." On your day off you should cease to do those things that are part of your normal work load. Give yourself a break and do only those things that help you relax and feel refreshed.

On my day off, for example, I try to avoid anything and everything that involves normal work. I only read books that are non-work related. I don't check my email on my day off, and my wife and I don't answer our business phone. My wife and I have both agreed not to talk about stressful, work-related topics between ourselves on our day off. I want to rest my mind—not engage it with the problems and stresses of the other six days. I do sleep a lot, take walks, and enjoy family, food, and anything that is restful.

HEALTHY MARRIAGE

Those leading youth need to maintain a healthy marriage if they're going to maintain a healthy ministry. Karen Hutchcraft, veteran of youth ministry with her husband Ron, writes,

One of the major lessons I learned early in our youth-work partnership is that an effective ministry is a by-product of a secure marriage. Youth workers are often underappreciated and over criticized. They are besieged with impossible expectations. All that can be pretty rough on the ego. When a youth leader walks into his home, he doesn't need another battleground where he has to defend or promote something. What he needs at home is a safe sanctuary.[76]

The following article appeared in one of the earliest editions of The Wittenberg Door. It's a chilling reminder for youth ministers to prioritize those closest to them.

My husband is a full-time youth minister. He is extremely dedicated and spends between 50 and 70 hours a week with young people.

I think the reason he is so successful with kids is that he is always available to them, always ready to help when they need him.

That may be the reason why the attendance has more than doubled in the past year. He really knows how to talk their language. This past year, he would be out two and three nights a week talking with kids until midnight. He's always taking them to camps and ski-trips and overnight campouts. If he isn't with the kids, he's thinking about them and preparing for his next encounter with them.

And, if he has any time left after that, he is speaking or attending a conference where he can share with others what God is doing through him. When it comes to youth work, my husband has always been 100 percent.

I guess that's why I left him.

There isn't much left after 100 percent.

Frankly, I just couldn't compete with "God." I say that because my husband always had a way of reminding me that this was God's work, and he must minister where and when God called him. Young people desperately needed help, and God had called him to help them. When a young person needed him, he had to respond or he would be letting God and the young person down.

When I did ask my husband to spend some time with the kids or me, it was always tentative, and if I became pushy about it, I was "nagging," "trying to get him out of God's work," "behaving selfishly," or I was revealing a "spiritual problem."

Honestly, I never wanted anything but God's will for my husband, but I never could get him to consider that maybe his family was part of that will.

It didn't matter how many discussions we had about his schedule, he would always end with "Okay, I'll get out of the ministry if that's what you want." Of course, I didn't want that, so we would continue as always until another discussion.

You can only ask for so long. There is a limit to how long you can be ignored and put off. You threaten to leave without meaning it until you keep the threat. You consider all the unpleasant consequences until they don't seem unpleasant anymore. You decide that nothing could be more unpleasant than being alone and feeling worthless.

You finally make up your mind that you are a person with real worth as an individual. You assert your ego and join womanhood again.

That's what I did.

I wanted to be more than a housekeeper, diaper changer, and sex partner. I wanted to be free from the deep bitterness and guilt that slowly ate at my spiritual and psychological sanity.

Deep inside there was something making me dislike not only my husband, but everything he did or touched.

His "I love you" became meaningless to me because he didn't act like it. His gifts were evidence to me of his guilt because he didn't spend more time with me. His sexual advances were met with a frigidity that frustrated both of us and deepened the gap between us.

All I wanted was to feel as though he really wanted to be with me. But, no matter how hard I tried, I always felt like I was keeping him from something. He had a way of making me feel guilty because I had forced him to spend his valuable time with the kids and myself.

Just once I wish he would have canceled something for us instead of canceling us.

You don't have to believe this, but I really loved him and his ministry once. I never wanted him to work an eight-to-five job. Nor did I expect him to be home every night. I tried to believe every promise he made me, honestly hoping things would change, but they never did.

All of a sudden I woke up one day and realized that I had become a terribly bitter person. I not only resented my husband and his work, but I was beginning to despise myself. In desperation to save myself, our children, and I guess, even my husband and his ministry, I left him.

I don't think he really believed I'd leave him. I guess I never really believed I'd leave him either. But I did.[77]

A youth leader needs to make sure that his or her spouse is the number one priority and best friend. This means praying together on a regular basis and not keeping secrets from one another. When the youth leader stumbles in any area of life, the spouse should be the first one to confess to. Such accountability protects the youth leader and makes him or her more effective in youth ministry.

PRIORITIZING FAMILY

Youth ministers can't be available to everyone. They need to place boundaries around what they can and cannot do. Students will wait. The most important priority is spouse and family. One reason youth ministers don't stay long in one church is because of crazy schedules that destroy family life. Duffy Robbins writes,

> Family life is not as easy as youth ministry. To be frank, it is much easier to be a good youth worker than it is to be a good father and husband or a good mother and wife. I can give the youth group kids all kinds of counsel about all kinds of topics, but when the situation turns dirty, I have the option of walking away from the problem. I can plead that the situation has grown beyond my expertise or responsibility. Not so with my family. It is always easier to work through other people's problems than it is to work through my own. It's sort of like the old maxim: Minor surgery is when they operate on you; major surgery is when they operate on me.[78]

As I travel around the world, I often meet pastors who are mourning one or more children who are no longer following Jesus. I grieve with and for these pastors. I also rejoice to hear of children who have come back to Jesus because of the parent's willingness to change. I talked with one missionary who told me that his dad, an international minister, stopped his ministry for one year to spend time with him during his troubled years. I admire this father's commitment to place the well-being of his child above his own ministerial success. Sadly, many have prioritized their own success in ministry over their children and suffer later on when their children walk away from Jesus.

The family quiet time is the best time for parents to nurture children in the ways of God and prepare them for life with Christ. I strongly believe that the family altar should be a daily priority when the children are young. Yet, growing godly, healthy kids isn't only about shared devotional time. It's also about friendship, fun, spontaneous activity. Plato once wrote,

"You can learn more about a man in an hour of play than in a year of conversation."[79]

Children feel cared for and loved when the husband and wife live in harmony. An intimate relationship between husband and wife is half the battle when it comes to child-rearing. The husband and wife relationship is the glue that makes the other relationships work. The greatest thing a father can do for his children is to love his wife and conversely that the wife respects the husband.

CONNECTED TO THE VINE

Christ's hidden life within will bear fruit in youth ministry. Jesus called himself the vine and told his followers to remain in him in order to bring forth fruit (John 15). While spiritual closeness to Jesus is the number one priority, the inner family circle of wife and children are a close second. More important than youth ministry fruit is spouse and family success.

A strong youth ministry flows from a healthy marriage and family. In fact, it's usually the carnal pressures to produce that cause youth leaders to think they must forsake the most important disciplines to "do" the work of the ministry. This is simply not true. The good news is that wrong thinking can always be righted and mistakes made in youth ministry can always be corrected. Proverbs 24:16 says, "For though a righteous man falls seven times, he rises again, but the wicked are brought down by calamity."

_____Chapter 12_____
MISTAKES IN YOUTH CELL MINISTRY

When Thomas Edison invented the light bulb, he tried over 2,000 experiments before he got it to work. A young reporter asked him how it felt to fail so many times. He replied, "I never failed once. It just happened to be a 2,000-step process." When people try something new, they rarely get things right the first or even second time—and often mistakes are still made after three or four more attempts. In fact, human beings grow and mature through trial and error.

We think of Peter as the great apostle and leader in the early church, but we forget how he arrived at that place. One key reason is that he was willing to step out of the boat and try. Yes, he failed. He sank. But at least he tried. There were eleven bigger failures sitting in the boat. The worst failure is not to sink but to fail to get out of the boat. We all make mistakes

(James 3:2). The key to success is to learn from mistakes and not to allow discouragement of mistakes to take control.

As you read this chapter, you might identify with some of the mistakes made in youth ministry. The most important thing is to learn from the mistakes. As more than one person has said, "We need to learn to fail forward."

CONFLICT WITH THE LEAD PASTOR

Although team ministry is the norm of the New Testament, one person has to be responsible to make the final call. In the local church, this person is the lead pastor. Yes, there's always the possibility that the youth pastor plants a new church and assumes the lead pastor role, but until that happens, the youth pastor must be fully supportive and encouraging of the lead pastor's vision.

The lead pastor has a lot of concerns and burdens. It's not the place of the youth worker to add to those concerns. The lead pastor has taken on the youth worker as part of his team and that investment should not be burdensome.

Youth workers can falter when they expect too much attention, more money, or begin to gossip about the "problems in the church." By demanding attention and complaining for the lack of it, the youth leader is opening up the door to a quick departure.

Youth pastors can and should share transparently with the lead pastor. This means being open to talk about difficulties and struggles. But there comes a point in which the youth pastor becomes a drain and a weight. Youth workers should not take every problem to the lead pastor, but rather should be mature enough to deal with the majority of problems themselves, while leaving the main issues for help from the lead pastor.

It helps if the youth pastor can develop his own team to help carry the burden of youth ministry—like Moses and the seventy elders who helped carry his load (Numbers 11:25). Doug Fields counsels, "Be strategic about when you ask your senior pastor to persuade others concerning youth ministry issues or needs."[80]

Youth workers need to be encouragers. "Great job, pastor. Good sermon." Encouragement is oxygen to the soul and lead pastors need a lot of it. Positive, upbeat youth workers can avoid many problems and roadblocks.

Avoid all gossip or bad-mouthing of the lead pastor and refuse to engage other youth who are gossiping. Some youth might approach the youth leader saying, "How come the pastor isn't more relevant in his sermons. He is so boring. I don't want to attend the Sunday message." The youth worker needs to deflect all such criticism, telling the person that such conversation is biblically inappropriate and suggesting that the person share his personal concerns directly with the lead pastor.

When unresolvable conflict does occur, it's essential that the youth worker follows the counsel of Christ laid out in Matthew 18:15-17 and goes directly to the lead pastor with those conflicts.

Thankfulness in everything and a diligent prayer life is greatly needed in youth ministry. The verse in Philippians 4:6 should hang on each youth leader's wall, "Do not be anxious about anything, but in every situation, by prayer and petition, with thanksgiving, present your requests to God."

BEING OVERLY CONCERNED ABOUT SIZE

When my children were teenagers, they loved to go to Christian concerts, featuring contemporary Christian bands. One time we went to an event called Spirit West Coast, a three day gathering of various bands. Day after day, we gathered with thousands of others to hear famous artists play their music. There's something electric about a large crowd, a coming together of a lot of people in one place.

Jesus attracted crowds, but he was seeking long-term personal commitments (Mt 23:37), not temporary relief because of the miracles he performed. Unless the crowd embraces core biblical truths, true discipleship rarely happens. The reality is that there is no direct correlation between crowd size and whether those in the crowd are becoming disciples of Jesus.

Jesus ministered to the crowd but focused on his small group of disciples. Michael Wilkins dedicated his life to understand the meaning of discipleship. His main textbook on discipleship, *Following the Master*, is the most exhaustive on the subject. He writes, "The objective of Jesus' ministry among the crowd was to make them disciples. As he taught and preached, the sign of faith was when one came out of the crowd and called Jesus 'Lord' (Mt 8:18-21)."[81]

Often youth ministries are bent on maximizing Disney-like experiences. Everything needs to be perfectly synced to ensure that people come back. The planning shouts loudly that there is one goal in mind: attract and keep young people in the youth service. David Kinnaman and Aly Hawkins in their ground-breaking book, *You Lost Me*, give a wide variety of reasons why young people are leaving the church today. One reason is being too attached to numbers. They write,

A fourth practice that contributes to shallow faith is the fact that many of our youth ministries fixate on numbers of attendees rather than measuring spiritual growth and transformation . . . some large youth groups actually do damage to young souls by taking the "factory" approach to faith development.[82]

Many churches expect the youth pastor to provide a busy schedule full of events to keep the youth coming back each week. After all, the church down the street has a full calendar of events, retreats, and programs. The temptation is to feel pressured to keep the numbers strong. Sadly, many youth ministers either leave the ministry or are asked to leave because of failure to grow the size of the youth group. Ray Johnston writes,

Another barrier is the love affair we have with the size of the youth ministry. Find any gathering of youth workers and the number one question asked is usually, "how many kids do you have in your youth group?" Many of us do not realize that if we have more than a handful of kids we may have more that we could ever develop. Jesus spent the better part of three years working full time with twelve people.[83]

If the size of the crowd is the goal, the youth leader can easily revert to programs rather than to developing disciples. Large events do have their place, but they should never be a substitute for intentional discipleship. The youth worker needs to always remember that the primary motivation is fulfilling the Great Commission to make disciples who make disciples.

NOT WORKING WITH PARENTS

If those in youth ministry plan to effectively minister to students over the long-haul, they need to humbly ask parents to be involved in the process. After all, the primary youth ministers are not church workers; they are parents. Moses is talking to parents when he says in Deuteronomy 6:5-7, "These commandments that I give you today are to be upon your hearts. Impress them on your children. Talk about them when you sit at home and when you walk along the road, when you lie down and when you get up."

Parents have a head-start in teaching their children from an early age through devotions, Bible memorization, and especially exemplifying the Christian life in a meaningful way. Biblical scholar Patrick Miller writes about Deuteronomy chapter six:

> The picture [provided here] is that of a family continually in lively conversation about the meaning of their experience with God and God's expectations of them. Parental teaching of the children by conversation about "the words," study of God's instruction, and reflection on it (cf. Ps. 1:2 and Josh. 1:8) is to go on in the family and the community . . . parents should teach their children in such a way that their last thoughts before falling asleep and their first words upon getting up are about the Lord's command.[84]

Research confirms that parents have the most spiritual influence on their children, and the greatest potential of ensuring their children stay close to God. The "National Study of Youth and Religion" concluded that, generally speaking, young persons will end up following the same religious path as their parents.[85]

Youth leaders need to realize that the few hours he or she spends with a young person each week cannot offset the many years of informal education amassed by that young person as he observes his mother and father. Parents have spent a life with the person. The reality is that parents are far more influential in a young persons's healthy development than any other single external influence. Peer influence, though powerful, runs a distant second in influence to the impact of parents.[86]

And parents make great helpers in youth ministry, if they are willing to develop relationships with youth, respect youth in their process of development, and enter their world.

Cypress Creek Church has dynamic junior high and high school youth cells. I noticed the junior high boys praying for one another, ministering God's Word, and just having a fun, dynamic time. I also noticed that the adult hosts were there to greet the boys and even played sports with them before the cell group activity began. In other words, the adults were committed and passionate about the youth cell vision, willing to open their homes, and serve as mentors to the youth.

The parental commitment at Cypress Creek didn't happen overnight. It took carefully nurturing by Rob Campbell and the pastoral team. Yet, even in a cell church like Cypress Creek, some parents might be new and need help to understand why it's important to meet in youth cells. Youth workers need to gracefully ask for their help and involvement to make cell ministry successful over the long-haul.

LACK OF CONSISTENCY

We met Blake Foster, youth pastor at Antioch Community Church in Waco, Texas, in an earlier chapter. Foster discovered that a huge problem among youth today is consistency. "What young people are looking for today is consistency," he told me. "If the leader simply shows up, youth are more than ready to offer lots of grace."

Youth pastors tend to come and go. They're ready to change the world, but then they may leave just as quickly because a new, better opportunity opens up somewhere else. Those who are effective with youth stay long enough to get to know the youth, gain their trust, and have significant ministry time with the same youth. It takes a while for the youth to develop a meaningful relationship with the youth minister.

It's not the bravado, the show, or a first impression. The reality is that youth can quickly see through facades and superficiality. They are looking for reality. They are looking for commitment, something that many of them haven't seen in their own families.

Much of the problem stems from the inconsistency of adults in general. Many parents simply walk away and divorce when problems surface. The destruction caused in the children and youth are incalculable. When adults are inconsistent, the youth feel it.

It's not easy to hang in there over the long haul. Foster said to me, "Youth ministry is unglamorous work. Youth ministry can often be a punching bag. When there's a problem, youth ministry is often the closest person to blame. A person should never go into youth ministry for the praise of man."

Consistency is more important than personality. Rather, than trying to be someone else, fruitful, consistent youth ministers choose to be themselves. Those ministering to youth need to be willing to be transparent and express their own emotions. Youth worker, Tim Smith says, "Teens are emotional, and they are looking for adults who know how to deal with their emotions. Denying we have emotions like fear, doubt, anger, and sadness robs us of the opportunity to build bridges into the hearts of the teens in our groups."[87] Perhaps the phrase "consistent transparency" is the best way to put it. Whether quiet, outgoing, intellectual, or passionate, the youth leader needs to be himself, willing to share openly and transparently.

NOT PRAYING

Paul wrote the Colossian epistle at the end of his life, and it's noteworthy that one of his final exhortations was about prayer. He said, "Devote yourselves to prayer, being watchful and thankful" (Colossians 4:2). The Greek word for devote literally means to attend constantly. To illustrate his point, Paul uses the example of Epaphras, ". . . who is always wrestling in prayer for you, that you may stand firm in all the will of God, mature and fully assured" (Colossians 4:12). Epaphras labored fervently and constantly for the believers in Colossae. We must continually cry out, "Lord, make us like Epaphras!" Commitment to prayer is the arsenal that God has given to his entire body of believers. And it's the most important weapon God has given the Church to win souls and make disciples.

The reality is that youth ministry is spiritual warfare. Satan and his demonic following would prefer that the church not prioritize youth. The enemy of our souls does not want to see youth formed by the Spirit of God. If the church is not praying, the battle will be too fierce, the devil will deceive too readily. We must not forget the importance of prayer. It is all important.

Youth ministries that prioritize prayer realize that only God can make disciples of the next generation. It's a myth to rely only on books, techniques, or even experience in developing youth. Only God can provide sustained growth and protection. Commitment to prayer allows us to rely on God himself for wisdom and direction. It teaches us to depend on him to discover the best way to develop youth or get the parents involved.

Only through prayer can the church break down cultural resistance and live New Testament lifestyles in community with one another. Only through prayer and an emphasis on spirituality will members be willing to dedicate volunteer time to prepare the future generation now.

True success in youth ministry comes from God. If we are going to make disciples of the next generation, we need to do it through the blessing of almighty God upon the congregation. God spoke to Jeremiah saying, "But let him who boasts boast about this: that he understands and knows me, that I am the LORD, who exercises kindness, justice and righteousness on earth, for in these I delight," (Jeremiah 9:24).

Those who lead youth and develop the next generation need to possess the essential characteristic of dependence on God, along with the knowledge and practice of diligent prayer. Other leadership characteristics can help, but spirituality is the chief requirement.

Chapter 13
CONCLUSION

In his later years, king David wrote, "I was young and now I am old, yet I have never seen the righteous forsaken or their children begging bread" (Psalm 37:25). David as an older man, reflected back on his youth and remembered God's faithfulness.

In the introduction to this book, I wrote about my own experience of becoming Christ's disciple in a youth cell when I was nineteen years old and how that involvement set a pattern for cell ministry and research that continues to this present time. Upon the writing of this book, I turned sixty. While I don't feel "old," I do realize I'm not getting any younger, and I can relate to the psalmist's words "I was young and now I am old." Time has flown by.

The next generation is preparing to take the leadership baton, and like it or not, we in the current generation will have to pass the baton to them. But will they be prepared? Will the youth today know how to lead the church of tomorrow? Or will they continue to promote paradigms which fail to fulfill Christ's Great Commission of making disciples who make disciples.

In the pages of this book, we've met churches, leaders, and writers who believe that youth are the future of the church and cell ministry is biblical and strategic in forming them to lead the next generation. We've looked at churches who are effectively handing the baton to young people and preparing them to make disciples in today's church through cell ministry.

Youth are full of dreams and goals and have the necessary energy to fulfill them. God has made them that way. God is raising up a new generation of youth to fulfill the Great Commission, and we who are older have the opportunity to not only cheer them but to also train them.

The church that develops the next generation will win tomorrow's battles. Youth cells give the next generation an opportunity to participate in significant ministry. They release youth through challenging ministry that can result in youth becoming the next generation of church planters and church leaders. Cell groups and cell churches provide the environment and incremental steps necessary to make disciples who make disciples. Youth in cell ministry is more than numbers. It is more than techniques and methodology. Youth in cell ministry is all about making disciples who will change the world.

As the church of the Twenty-First Century rises to effectively meet the challenges of youth in house to house ministry, a new generation of disciples will rise up, churches will be planted, missionaries will be sent forth, "and the gospel of the kingdom will be preached in the whole world as a testimony to all nations" until the Jesus comes again (Matthew 24:14).

Endnotes

1. In the Greek world, philosophers were surrounded by their pupils. The Jews claimed to be disciples of Moses (John 9:28) and the followers of John the Baptist were known as his disciples (Mark 2:18; John 1:35).

2. There is no indicator in Scripture of a specific age for any disciple, but the historical context gives clues. In the time of Jesus, a Jewish man received a wife after the age of 18. Ray VanderLaan gives various arguments for the young ages of the disciples here: https://kbonikowsky.wordpress.com/2008/08/20/jesus-disciples-a-teenage-posse/

3. Ron Hutchcraft, *The Battle for a Generation* (Chicago, IL: Moody Press, 1996), p. 20.

4. Ibid., p. 20.

5.   Brian Sauder and Sarah Mohler, compilers, *Youth Cells and Youth Ministry* (Ephrata, PA: House to House Publications, 2000), p. 56.

6.   Alex and Brett Harris, *Do Hard Things: A Teenage Rebellion Against Low Expectations* (Colorado Springs, CO: Multnomah Books, 2008), p. 12.

7.   Kara Eckmann Powell, "Chapter 12: Focusing Youth Ministry through Community," in Kenda Creasy Dean, Chap Clark, Dave Rahn, editors, *Starting Right: Thinking Theologically about Youth Ministry* (Grand Rapids, MI: Zondervan Publishing House, 2001), p. 201.

8.   Personal email to me on June 10, 2016.

9.   George Ladd, *A Theology of the New Testament* (Grand Rapids, MI: Eerdmans, 1974), p. 545.

10.   Ginny Ward Holderness, *Teaming Up: Shared Leadership in Youth Ministry* (Louisville, KY: Westminster John Knox Press, 1997), p. 38.

11.   Kenda Creasy Dean, Chap Clark, Dave Rahn, editors, *Starting Right: Thinking Theologically about Youth Ministry* (Grand Rapids, MI: Zondervan Publishing House, 2001), p. 44.

12.   Mark H. Senter III, *When God Shows Up: A History of Protestant Youth Ministry in America* (Grand Rapids, MI: Baker Academics, 2010), p. 32.

13.   Chap Clark, "Chapter 2: The Changing Face of Adolescence: A Theological View of Human Development," Kenda Creasy Dean, Chap Clark, David Rahn, *Starting Right: Thinking Theologically about Youth Ministry* (Grand Rapids, MI: Zondervan Publishing House, 2001), p. 54.

14.   Steve Gerali, "Chapter 18: Seeing Clearly: Community Context," in Kenda Creasy Dean, Chap Clark, Dave Rahn, editors, *Starting Right: Thinking Theologically about Youth Ministry*

(Grand Rapids, MI: Zondervan Publishing House, 2001), p. 288.

15. Ibid., p. 288.

16. Troy Jones, *From Survival to Significance: The How Tos of Youth Ministry for the Twenty-First Century* (Mukilteo, WA: WinePress Publishing, 1998), pp. 23-29.

17. Robbins, Duffy (2009-08-30). *This Way to Youth Ministry: Companion Guide* (YS Academic) (Kindle Locations 5899-5908). Zondervan/Youth Specialties. Kindle edition.

18. According to the respected Kaiser Family Foundation (2010) report: "Today, 8-18 year-olds devote an average of 7 hours and 38 minutes to using entertainment media across a typical day (more than 53 hours a week). And because they spend so much of that time 'media multitasking' (using more than one medium at a time), they actually manage to pack in a total of 10 hours and 45 minutes' worth of media content into those 7 and ½ hours." According to the Kaiser report, young people are spending 25% of their online time with multiple media devises and 31% say that they are using multiple media while doing their homework (Kaiser Family Foundation, "Generation M2," as quoted in Dean Borgman, Foundations for Youth Ministry: Theological Engagement with Teen Life and Culture (Grand Rapids, MI: Baker Academic, 2013), p. 219.

19. As quoted in Duffy, Kindle Locations 3991-3994.

20. George Barna, "Teens and Adults Have Little Chance of Accepting Christ as Their Savior," The Barna Report (October-December 1999), n.p. as quoted in Jim Burns and Mike Devries, *Partnering with Parents in Youth Ministry* (Ventura, CA: Gospel Light, 2003), p. 13.

21. Hutchcraft, p. 35.

22. Brian Sauder and Sarah Mohler, compilers, *Youth Cells and Youth Ministry* (Ephrata, PA: House to House Publications, 2000), p. 24.

23. Christian Schwarz, *Natural Church Development* (Carol Steam, IL: ChurchSmart Resources), p. 31.

24. Wayne Rice, *Reinventing Youth Ministry* [Again] (Downers Grove, IL: InterVarsity Press, 2010), pp. 188-189.

25. Ibid., p. 189.

26. Kinnaman, David; Hawkins, Aly (2011-10-01). *You Lost Me: Why Young Christians Are Leaving Church . . . and Rethinking Faith* (Kindle Locations 3219-3226). Baker Publishing Group. Kindle Edition.

27. The Kids' Slot is when children from 4 to 12 leave the adult cell to have their own lesson. The children stay with the adults during the icebreaker and worship but then leave for their Bible teaching (Kids' Slot). Youth often lead this time in IG cells but at YAC the youth normally stay in the IG group and acts as normal participants.

28. Each week, the different zones meet separately in the church for Bible teaching (Tuesday, Wednesday, Thursday, and Friday). In each of these four services, the youth meet separately in an adjacent room and there are about eighty youth in each of these separate services.

29. Daphne Kirk wrote these words on "cellchurchtalk" on 1/1/2003.

30. Quote from Ralph Neighbour on "cellchurchtalk" in response to Daphne Kirk's comments about IG youth cells in 2003, although it seems I lost the exact email and so I don't have a specific date.

31. Philip Woolford [pkwool@iprimus.com.au] wrote to "cell-churchtalk" on Thursday, January 02, 2003.

32. Sauder and Mohler, p. 19.

33. Ibid., p. 20

34. Ibid., p. 98.

35. Ibid., p. 19.

36. Ibid., p. 20.

37. Ted Stump, "Student Led Cell Groups: Nothing Short of a Revolution," Published in *Youthworker Magazine*, September/October, 1998. Ted Stump is the founder and director of High Impact Ministries. He holds a Master of Divinity from Columbia Biblical Seminary. Ted's ministry experience includes study and travel with Dr. Ralph Neighbour, Jr., Josh McDowell, and evangelist John Guest. Ted serves as a national consultant to churches and youth organizations on developing and implementing student cell groups.

38. Ibid.

39. Ibid.

40. Personal email on Thursday, March 10, 2016.

41. Survey results courtesy of American Institute for Church Growth in Pasadena, California as quoted in Jimmy Seibert, Reaching College Students through Cells (Houston, TX: Touch Publications, 1997), p. 37.

42. Sauder and Mohler, p. 24.

43. Doug Fields, *Purpose Driven Youth Ministry: 9 Essential Foundations for Healthy Growth* (Grand Rapids, MI: Zondervan Publishing House, 1998), p. 152.

44. Accessed on Wednesday, July 27, 2016 at https://en.wikipedia.org/wiki/A_picture_is_worth_a_thousand_words

45. Now Vine asks children's cell leaders to be sixteen, but back then they didn't have that rule.

46. Because the Groups of Twelve movement in the International Charismatic Mission, led by César Castellanos, became increasingly model driven, I no longer promote G12 and have not done so since 2002.

47. César Fajardo, *The Vision,* audiotape of lecture presented at the Fourth Convention of Multiplication and Revival, January 1999.

48. "Tent of Meeting in Print," 4.

49. Mike Osborn, "The Heart behind Cells" *CellChurch* Vol. 8, no.1 (Winter 1999): 26.

50. "The Teenage Solider of World War One," BBC magazine, November 11, 2014. Accessed on Thursday, June 16, 2016 at http://www.bbc.com/news/magazine-29934965

51. "The Sixth Division," accessed on Thursday, June 16, 2016 at http://onesixthnet.yuku.com/topic/912/What-was-the-average-age-of-US-soldiers-in-WWII#.V2MB2vkrKVM

52. To learn more about the gifts of the Spirit I would recommend reading through the key Bible passages in Romans 12, 1 Corinthians 12-14, Ephesians 4, and 1 Peter 4. I would also encourage the leader and team to read books on the gifts of the Spirit (I've written two books on gifts in the small group). There are also a number spiritual gift tests available, and it would be a great idea to have the entire team take one of those gift tests—although I feel the best way to spot spiritual gifts is through relational observation and testing in the group.

53. Doug Fields, *Your First Two Years in Youth Ministry* (Grand Rapids, MI: Zondervan Publishing House, 2002), pp. 200-201.

54. Sauder and Mohler, p. 42.

55. John Ayot, *Dictionary of Word Origins,* "Coach" (New York: Arcade Publishing, 1990).

56. Jim Egli and Dwight Marble, *Small Groups, Big Impact* (Saint Charles, IL: Churchsmart Resources, 2011), p. 60.

57. Fields, *Purpose Driven Youth Ministry,* p. 190.

58. God revolutionized our lives in 1995 after reading Peter Wagner's book *Prayer Shield* (Ventura, CA: Regal Books, 1992). Both Celyce and I realized that it wasn't enough to send out "prayer letters" to friends. We needed to have specific prayer partners. One of the best ways to coach leaders is to encourage the leaders to have a prayer shield (those who are praying for the leader) and to be part of the prayer shield for the leader.

59. "Fresh Quotes," Accessed on Thursday, June 16, 2016 at http://www.thefreshquotes.com/youth-quotes/

60. Roger Thoman, "House Church Basics Pt. 7: What About Youth?" Written on March 18, 2004 and accessed on Thursday, December 11, 2014 at http://sojourner.typepad.com/house_church_blog/2004/03/house_church_ba_3.html .

61. Sauder and Mohler, p. 61.

62. Ibid.

63. John P. Kotter, *Leading Change* (Boston, MA: Harvard Business Press, 2012), pp. 288.

64. Sauder and Mohler, p. 60.

65. Senter III, Mark H.; Wesley Black; Chap Clark; Malan Nel (2010-01-05). *Four Views of Youth Ministry and the Church: Inclusive Congregational, Preparatory, Missional, Strategic* (YS Academic) (Kindle Locations 3586-3589). Zondervan Publishing House. Kindle Edition.

66. Ibid., Kindle Locations 3594-3608.

67. Jimmy Seibert, *Reaching College Students through Cells* (Houston, TX: Touch Publications, 1997), p. 9.

68. Ibid., p. 47.

69. "100 conferences" refers to some thirteen CCMN summits, approximately thirty missionary and international

conferences, and some sixty including regional, national, and coaching conferences.

70.   For more on this topic, read pp. 46-48 of *Natural Church Development* (Carol Stream, IL: ChurchSmart Resources, 1996).

71.   Jon Ireland, *Resolving Youth Workers Mistakes*, Fuller Doctor of Ministry Degree Dissertation (Pasadena, CA: Fuller Seminary, 1999), p. 17.

72.   Mike Yaconelli, *The Core Realities of Youth Ministry* (Grand Rapids, MI: Zondervan Publishing House, 2003), p. 109.

73.   Fields, *Purpose Driven Youth Ministry*, pp. 32-33.

74.   Ibid., p. 36.

75.   Morgan Lee, "Here's How 770 Pastors Describe Their Struggle with Porn," *Christianity Today* online, accessed on Thursday, January 28, 2016 at http://www.christianitytoday.com/gleanings/2016/january/how-pastors-struggle-porn-phenomenon-josh-mcdowell-barna.html

76.   As quoted in Paul Borthwick, *Feeding Your Forgotten Soul: Spiritual Growth for Youth Workers* (Grand Rapids, MI: Zondervan Publishing House, 1990), p. 106.

77.   The author was anonymous and this story appeared as "Diary of a Mad Housewife," in *The Wittenberg Door* (June 1971) as quoted in Robbins, Duffy (2009-08-30) *This Way to Youth Ministry: Companion Guide* (YS Academic) (Kindle Locations 3174-3219). Zondervan/Youth Specialties. Kindle edition.

78.   Robbins, Kindle Locations 3293-3298.

79.   Mike Mason, *The Practice of the Presence of People* (Colorado Springs, CO: Waterbrook Press, 1999), p. 106.

80.   Fields, *Your First Two Years in Youth Ministry*, p. 163.

81.   Michael J. Wilkins, *Following the Master* (Grand Rapids, MI: Zondervan Publishing House, 1992), p. 109.

82. Kinnaman, Hawkins, Kindle Locations 1932-1938.

83. Ray Johnston, *Developing Student Leaders* (Grand Rapids, MI: Zondervan Publishing House, 1992), p. 32.

84. Patrick D. Miller, *Deuteronomy—Interpretation: A Bible Commentary for Teaching and Preaching* (Louisville, KY: John Knox Press, 1990), pp. 107-108. See more at: http://fulleryouthinstitute.org/articles/is-youth-ministry-in-the-bible#sthash.CHZQe2BP.dpuf

85. Christian Smith and Melinda Lundquist Denton, *Soul Searching: The Religious and Spiritual Lives of American Teenagers* (Oxford, 2005), 261. See more at: http://fulleryouthinstitute.org/articles/is-youth-ministry-in-the-bible#sthash.CHZQe2BP.dpuf

86. Jim Burns and Mike Devries, *Partnering with Parents in Youth Ministry* (Grand Rapids, MI: Baker Publishing Group, 2003) point to a 2003 survey by Barna Research showed that seventy-eight percent of youth indicated that their parents had more influence on their decision making than anyone else in their lives.

87. Tim Smith, *8 Habits of an Effective Youth Worker* (Wheaton, IL: Victor Books, 1995), pp. 83-85.

.

_____ Resources _____

RESOURCES BY
JOEL COMISKEY

You can find all of Joel Comiskey's books
at Joel Comiskey Group

Phone: 1-888-511-9995

Website: www.joelcomiskeygroup.com

Joel Comiskey's previous books cover the following topics

- Leading a cell group (*How to Lead a Great Cell Group Meeting*, 2001, 2009; *Children in Cell Ministry*, 2016; *Youth in Cell Ministry*, 2016).

- How to multiply the cell group (*Home Cell Group Explosion*, 1998).

- How to prepare spiritually for cell ministry (*An Appointment with the King*, 2002, 2011).

- How to practically organize your cell system (*Reap the Harvest*, 1999; *Cell Church Explosion*, 2004).

- How to train future cell leaders (*Leadership Explosion*, 2001; *Live*, 2007; *Encounter*, 2007; *Grow*, 2007; *Share*, 2007; *Lead*, 2007; *Coach*, 2008; *Discover*, 2008).

- How to coach/care for cell leaders (*How to be a Great Cell Group Coach*, 2003; *Groups of Twelve*, 2000; *From Twelve to Three*, 2002).

- How the gifts of the Spirit work within the cell group (*The Spirit-filled Small Group*, 2005, 2009; *Discover*, 2008).

- How to fine tune your cell system (*Making Cell Groups Work Navigation Guide*, 2003).

- Principles from the second largest church in the world (*Passion and Persistence*, 2004).

- How cell church works in North America (*The Church that Multiplies*, 2007, 2009).

- How to plant a church (*Planting Churches that Reproduce*, 2009)

- How to be a relational disciple (*Relational Disciple*, 2010).

- How to distinguish truth from myths (*Myths and Truths of the Cell Church*, 2011).

- What the Biblical foundations for cell church are (*Biblical Foundations for the Cell-Based Church*, 2012, *Making Disciples in the Cell-Based Church*, 2013, *2000 Years of Small Groups*, 2015).

All of the books listed are available from Joel Comiskey Group
www.joelcomiskeygroup.com

How To Lead A Great Cell Group Meeting:
So People Want to Come Back

Do people expectantly return to your group meetings every week? Do you have fun and experience joy during your meetings? Is everyone participating in discussion and ministry? You can lead a great cell group meeting, one that is life changing and dynamic. Most people don't realize that they can create a God-filled atmosphere because they don't know how. Now the secret is out. This guide will show you how to:

- Prepare yourself spiritually to hear God during the meeting
- Structure the meeting so it flows
- Spur people in the group to participate and share their lives openly
- Share your life with others in the group
- Create stimulating questions
- Listen effectively to discover what is transpiring in others' lives
- Encourage and edify group members
- Open the group to non-Christians
- See the details that create a warm atmosphere

By implementing these time-tested ideas, your group meetings will become the hot-item of your members' week. They will go home wanting more and return each week bringing new people with them. 140 pgs.

Home Cell Group Explosion: How Your Small Group Can Grow and Multiply

The book crystallizes the author's findings in some eighteen areas of research, based on a meticulous questionnaire that he submitted to cell church leaders in eight countries around the world, locations that he also visited personally for his research. The detailed notes in the back of the book offer the student of cell church growth a rich mine for further reading. The beauty of Comiskey's book is that he not only summarizes his survey results in a thoroughly convincing way but goes on to analyze in practical ways many of his survey results in separate chapters. The happy result is that any cell church leader, intern or member completing this quick read will have his priorities/values clearly aligned and ready to be followed-up. If you are a pastor or small group leader, you should devour this book! It will encourage you and give you simple, practical steps for dynamic small group life and growth. 175 pgs.

An Appointment with the King: *Ideas for Jump-Starting Your Devotional Life*

With full calendars and long lists of things to do, people often put on hold life's most important goal: building an intimate relationship with God. Often, believers wish to pursue the goal but are not sure how to do it. They feel frustrated or guilty when their attempts at personal devotions seem empty and unfruitful. With warm, encouraging writing, Joel Comiskey guides readers on how to set a daily appointment with the King and make it an exciting time they will look forward to. This book first answers the question "Where do I start?" with step-by-step instructions on how to spend time with God and practical ideas for experiencing him more fully. Second, it highlights the benefits of spending time with God, including joy, victory over sin, and spiritual guidance. The book will help Christians tap into God's resources on a daily basis, so that even in the midst of busyness they can walk with him in intimacy and abundance. 175 pgs.

Reap the Harvest: *How a Small Group SysSystem Can Grow System Can Grow Your Church*

Have you tried small groups and hit a brick wall? Have you wondered why your groups are not producing the fruit that was promised? Are you looking to make your small groups more effective? Cell-church specialist and pastor Dr. Joel Comiskey studied the world's most successful cell churches to determine why they grow. The key: They have embraced specific principles. Conversely, churches that do not embrace these same principles have problems with their groups and therefore do not grow. Cell churches are successful not because they have small groups but because they can support the groups. In this book, you will discover how these systems work. 236 pgs.

La Explosión de la Iglesia Celular: *Cómo Estructurar la Iglesia en Células Eficaces* (Editorial Clie, 2004)

This book is available only in Spanish and contains Joel Comiskey's research of eight of the world's largest cell churches, five of which reside in Latin America. It details how to make the transition from a traditional church to the cell church structure and many other valuable insights, including: the history of the cell church, how to organize your church to become a praying church, the most important principles of the cell church, and how to raise up an army of cell leaders. 236 pgs.

Leadership Explosion: *Multiplying Cell Group Leaders to Reap the Harvest*

Some have said that cell groups are leader breeders. Yet even the best cell groups often have a leadership shortage. This shortage impedes growth and much of the harvest goes untouched. Joel Comiskey has discovered why some churches are better at raising up new cell leaders than others. These churches do more than pray and hope for new leaders. They have an intentional strategy, a plan that will quickly equip as many new leaders as possible. In this book, you will discover the training models these churches use to multiply leaders. You will discover the underlying principles of these models so that you can apply them. 202 pgs.

FIVE-BOOK EQUIPPING SERIES

#1: Live   #2: Encounter   #3: Grow   #4: Share   #5: Lead

The five book equipping series is designed to train a new believer all the way to leading his or her own cell group. Each of the five books contains eight lessons. Each lesson has interactive activities that helps the trainee reflect on the lesson in a personal, practical way.

Live starts the training by covering key Christian doctrines, including baptism and the Lord's supper. 85 pgs.
Encounter guides the believer to receive freedom from sinful bondages. The Encounter book can be used one-on-one or in a group. 91 pgs.
Grow gives step-by-step instruction for having a daily quiet time, so that the believer will be able to feed him or herself through spending daily time with God. 87 pgs.
Share instructs the believer how to communicate the gospel message in a winsome, personal way. This book also has two chapters on small group evangelism. 91 pgs.
Lead prepares the Christian on how to facilitate an effective cell group. This book would be great for those who form part of a small group team. 91 pgs.

TWO-BOOK ADVANCED TRAINING SERIES

Coach   Discover

Coach and **Discover** make-up the Advanced Training, prepared specifically to take a believer to the next level of maturity in Christ.

Coach prepares a believer to coach another cell leader. Those experienced in cell ministry often lack understanding on how to coach someone else. This book provides step-by-step instruction on how to coach a new cell leader from the first meeting all the way to giving birth to a new group. The book is divided into eight lessons, which are interactive and help the potential coach deal with real-life, practical coaching issues. 85 pgs.

Discover clarifies the twenty gifts of the Spirit mentioned in the New Testament. The second part shows the believer how to find and use his or her particular gift. This book is excellent to equip cell leaders to discover the giftedness of each member in the group. 91 pgs.

How to be a Great Cell Group Coach: *Practical insight for Supporting and Mentoring Cell Group Leaders*

Research has proven that the greatest contributor to cell group success is the quality of coaching provided for cell group leaders. Many are serving in the position of a coach, but they don't fully understand what they are supposed to do in this position. Joel Comiskey has identified seven habits of great cell group coaches. These include: Receiving from God, Listening to the needs of the cell group leader, Encouraging the cell group leader, Caring for the multiple aspects of a leader's life, Developing the cell leader in various aspects of leadership, Strategizing with the cell leader to create a plan, Challenging the cell leader to grow.

Practical insights on how to develop these seven habits are outlined in section one. Section two addresses how to polish your skills as a coach with instructions on diagnosing problems in a cell group, how to lead coaching meetings, and what to do when visiting a cell group meeting. This book will prepare you to be a great cell group coach, one who mentors, supports, and guides cell group leaders into great ministry. 139 pgs.

Groups of Twelve: *A New Way to Mobilize Leaders and Multiply Groups in Your Church*

This book clears the confusion about the Groups of 12 model. Joel dug deeply into the International Charismatic Mission in Bogota, Colombia and other G12 churches to learn the simple principles that G12 has to offer your church. This book also contrasts the G12 model with the classic 5x5 and shows you what to do with this new model of ministry. Through onsite research, international case studies, and practical experience, Joel Comiskey outlines the G12 principles that your church can use today.

Billy Hornsby, director of the Association of Related Churches, says, "Joel Comiskey shares insights as a leader who has himself raised up numerous leaders. From how to recognize potential leaders to cell leader training to time-tested principles of leadership—this book has it all. The accurate comparisons of various training models make it a great resource for those who desire more leaders. Great book!" 182 pgs.

From Twelve To Three: *How to Apply G12 Principles in Your Church*

The concept of the Groups of 12 began in Bogota, Colombia, but now it is sweeping the globe. Joel Comiskey has spent years researching the G12 structure and the principles behind it.

From his experience as a pastor, trainer, and consultant, he has discovered that there are two ways to embrace the G12 concept: adopting the entire model or applying the principles that support the model.

This book focuses on the application of principles rather than adoption of the entire model. It outlines the principles and provides a modified application which Joel calls the G12.3. This approach presents a pattern that is adaptable to many different church contexts.

The concluding section illustrates how to implement the G12.3 in various kinds of churches, including church plants, small churches, large churches, and churches that already have cells. 178 pgs.

The Spirit-filled Small Group: Leading Your Group to Experience the Spiritual Gifts.

The focus in many of today's small groups has shifted from Spirit-led transformation to just another teacher-student Bible study. But exercising every member's spiritual gifts is vital to the effectiveness of the group. With insight born of experience in more than twenty years of small group ministry, Joel Comiskey explains how leaders and participants alike can be supernaturally equipped to deal with real-life issues. Put these principles into practice and your small group will never be the same!

This book works well with Comiskey's training book, **Discover.** It fleshes out many of the principles in Comiskey's training book. Chuck Crismier, radio host, *Viewpoint,* writes, "Joel Comiskey has again provided the Body of Christ with an important tool to see God's Kingdom revealed in and through small groups." 191 pgs.

Making Cell Groups Work Navigation Guide: *A Toolbox of Ideas and Strategies for Transforming Your Church.*

For the first time, experts in cell group ministry have come together to provide you with a page reference tool like no other. When Ralph Neighbour, Bill Beckham, Joel Comiskey and Randall Neighbour compiled new articles and information under careful orchestration and in-depth understanding that Scott Boren brings to the table, it's as powerful as private consulting! Joel Comiskey has an entire book within this mammoth page work. There are also four additional authors.

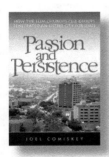

Passion and Persistence: *How the Elim Church's Cell Groups Penetrated an Entire City for Jesus*

This book describes how the Elim Church in San Salvador grew from a small group to 116,000 people in 10,000 cell groups. Comiskey takes the principles from Elim and applies them to churches in North America and all over the world. Ralph Neighbour says: "I believe this book will be remember as one of the most important ever written about a cell church movement! I experienced the passion when visiting Elim many years ago. Comiskey's report about Elim is not a pattern to be slavishly copied. It is a journey into grasping the true theology and methodology of the New Testament church. You'll discover how the Elim Church fans into flame their passion for Jesus and His Word, how they organize their cells to penetrate a city and world for Jesus, and how they persist until God brings the fruit." 158 pgs.

The Church that Multiplies: *Growing a Healthy Cell Church in North America*

Does the cell church strategy work in North America? We hear about exciting cell churches in Colombia and Korea, but where are the dynamic North American cell churches? This book not only declares that the cell church concept does work in North America but dedicates an entire chapter to examining North American churches that are successfully using the cell strategy to grow in quality and quantity. This book provides the latest statistical research about the North American church and explains why the cell church approach restores health and growth to the church today. More than anything else, this book will provide practical solutions for pastors and lay leaders to use in implementing cell-based ministry. 181 pgs.

Planting Churches that Reproduce: *Planting a Network of Simple Churches*

What is the best way to plant churches in the 21st century? Comiskey believes that simple, reproducible church planting is most effective. The key is to plant churches that are simple enough to grow into a movement of churches. Comiskey has been gathering material for this book for the past fifteen Years. He has also planted three churches in a wide variety of settings. Planting Churches that Reproduce is the fruit of his research and personal experience. Comiskey uses the latest North American church planting statistics, but extends the illustrations to include worldwide church planting. More than anything else, this book will provide practical solutions for those planting churches today. Comiskey's book is a must-read book for all those interested in establishing Christ-honoring, multiplying churches. 176 pgs.

The Relational Disciple: *How God Uses Community to Shape Followers of Jesus*

Jesus lived with His disciples for three years and taught them life lessons as a group. After three years, he commanded them to "go and do likewise" (Matthew 28:18-20). Jesus discipled His followers through relationships—and He wants us to do the same. Scripture is full of exhortations to love and serve one another. This book will show you how. The isolation present in the western world is creating a hunger for community and the world is longing to see relational disciples in action. This book will encourage Christ-followers to allow God to use the natural relationships in life—family, friends, work relationships, cells, church, and missions to mold them into relational disciples.

You Can Coach: *How to Help Leaders Build Healthy Churches through Coaching*

We've entitled this book "You Can Coach" because we believe that coaching is more about passing on what you've lived and holding others accountable in the process. Coaching doesn't require a higher degree, special talent, unique personality, or a particular spiritual gift. We believe, in fact, that God wants coaching to become a movement. We long to see the day in which every pastor has a coach and in turn is coaching someone else. In this book, you'll hear three coaches who have successfully coached pastors for many years. They will share their history, dreams, principles, and what God is doing through coaching. Our hope is that you'll be both inspired and resourced to continue your own coaching ministry in the years to come.

Myths & Truths of the Cell Church: *Key Principles that Make or Break Cell Ministry*

Most of the modern day cell church movement is dynamic, positive, and applicable. As is true in most endeavors, errors and false assumptions have also cropped up to destroy an otherwise healthy movement. Sometimes these false concepts caused the church to go astray completely. At other times, they led the pastor and church down a dead-end road of fruitless ministry. Regardless of how the myths were generated, they had a chilling effect on the church's ministry. In this book, Joel Comiskey tackles these errors and false assumptions, helping pastors and leaders to untangle the webs of legalism that has crept into the cell church movement. Joel then guides the readers to apply biblical, time-tested principles that will guide them into fruitful cell ministry. Each chapter begins with a unique twist. Well-known worldwide cell church leaders open each chapter by answering questions to the chapter's topic in the form of an email dialogue. Whether you're starting out for the first time in cell ministry or a seasoned veteran, this book will give you the tools to help your ministry stay fresh and fruitful.

Biblical Foundations for the Cell-Based Church

Why cell church? Is it because David Cho's church is a cell church and happens to be the largest church in the history of Christianity? Is it because cell church is the strategy that many "great" churches are using?

Ralph Neighbour repeatedly says, "Theology must breed methodology." Joel Comiskey has arrived at the same conclusion. Biblical truth is the only firm foundation for anything we do. Without a biblical base, we don't have a strong under-pinning upon which we can hang our ministry and philosophy. We can plod through most anything when we know that God is stirring us to behave biblically.

Making Disciples in the Cell-Based Church

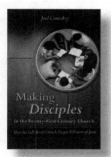

The primary goal of the church is to make disciples who make disciples. But how is the church supposed to do that? This book answers that question. Dr. Comiskey explains how both cell and celebration (larger gathering) work together in the process of making disciples. In the cell, a potential disciple is transformed through community, priesthood of all believers, group evangelism, and team multiplication. The cell system ensures each leader has a coach and that training happens. Then the cells gather together to worship and grow through the teaching of God's Word. This book will help you understand why and how to become a church that prioritizes discipleship.

What others are saying: I've read all of Joel Comiskey's books, but this one is his best work yet. I'm looking forward to having all of our pastors, coaches, cell leaders and members read this book in the near future. *Dr. Dennis Watson, Lead Pastor, Celebration Church of New Orleans*

I am so excited about Joel Comiskey's new book, Making Disciples in the Twenty-First Century Church. Joel has unpacked discipleship, not just as an endeavor for individuals, but as the critical element for creating a church community and culture that reproduces the Kingdom of God all over the earth. *Jimmy Seibert, Senior Pastor, Antioch Community Church* Like Joel's other books, this one is solidly biblical, highly practical, wonderfully accessible and is grounded in Joel's vast research and experience. *Dr. Dave Earley, Lead Pastor, Grace City Church of Las Vegas, Nevada*

2000 Years of Small Groups: A History of Cell Ministry in the Church

This book explores how God has used small groups through-out church history, specifically focusing on the early church to the present time. God not only established the early church as a house to house movement, but he also has used small groups throughout church history. This book chronicles the small group or cell movement from Jesus all the way to the modern day cell explosion. Themes include:Small Groups In Biblical History, Small Groups In Early Christian History, Small Groups and Monasticism, Small Groups During the Pre-Reformation Period, Luther and Small Groups, Martin Bucer and Small Groups, The Anabaptist Movement, Puritan Conventicles, Pietism, The Moravians, The Methodists, Modern House Churches, Small Groups in North America, and The Modern Day Cell Church. This book will both critique the strengths and weaknesses of these historical movements and apply principles to today's church.

Children in Cell Ministry: Discipling the Future Generation Now

Joel Comiskey challenges pastors and leaders to move from simply educating children to forming them into disciples who make disciples. Comiskey lays out the Biblical base for chil-dren's ministry and then encourages pastors and leaders to formulate their own vision and philosophy for ministry to chil-dren based on the Biblical text. Comiskey highlights how to disciple children in both the large group and the small group. He quickly moves into practical examples of intergenerational cell groups and how effective cell churches have implemented this type of group. He then writes about children only cell groups, citing many practical examples from some of the most effective cell churches in the world. Comiskey covers equipping for children, how to equip the parents, and mistakes in working with children in the cell church. This book will help those wanting to minister to children both in large and small groups. rch.

INDEX

V

W

Y

CPSIA information can be obtained
at www.ICGtesting.com
Printed in the USA
FSHW022103051118
53579FS